Christian Women's Service

◇◇◇◇◇◇◇◇◇◇◇◇◇◇◇

A Collection of Ministry Regarding the Place of Christian Women in Today's World

The Scriptures used throughout are both from the King James Version and the Darby Translation of the Bible.

Edited and assembled by: W. S. Chellberg
April 2020

ISBN : 978-0-912868-24-0

Published by --

BIBLES, etc.
Wheaton, IL USA

www.bibles-etc.com

Printed by --

LuLu Press
USA - France - Italy

www.lulu.com

PREFACE

We live in a world where it is considered to be an advancement of civilization to over-ride God's order for men and women. It is thought to be a good thing to give a woman the place of a man – you will have heard of such movements as Women's Liberation, Women's Rights, Women's Suffrage. It was Adam to whom God gave the job of naming the anmals, but it was not given to a man to give birth to the Messiah. Men and women each have their own distinct glory and it cannot be exchanged for the other.

This book is a collection of writings, addresses (sermons), and excerpts that we hope will be useful for Christian women (sisters). It has been our attempt to show that Christian men and women are equals in spiritual things, yet although the men bear the responsibility of acting and speaking publicly, women are to fill out their spiritual place as much as men according to the place they are given. It has been recorded for all generations to see that Adam bore the responsibility for sinning, and yet Eve was first in the transgression.

We would encourage additional reading and prayer. Each article and excerpt has the location of the original source so that, in the case of an excerpt, the context can be studied.

I have been aided by several others, especially several sisters, including my dear wife and daughter-in-law for which I thank. I now pass this collection into your hands having prayed that the Lord Jesus will bless it to you and will help you be everything that He wants you to be. So that you can fill out your place in the testimony to His praise and glory.

W.S.Chellberg
April 2020

TABLE of CONTENTS

--oooOOOooo--

Blessed is he that reads, and they that hear the words of the prophecy, and keep the things written in it; for the time is near.

Revelation 1:3

--oooOOOooo--

The Elder Women

The influence of "Elder women" for good or bad is great. Timothy was to regard them as "mothers." In the Epistle to Titus they are exhorted to teach the younger women. Not teach them as to doctrine exactly, but as to conduct, practice, to refer to instances where good influence was apparent it may suffice to name Anna in Luke 2; Phoebe in Romans 16; Chloe 1 Corinthians 1; Lois and Eunice in 2 Timothy; Moses' mother in Exodus 2; and Deborah in Judges. There are many others. Unhappily there are cases quite the reverse where the influence was evil. Delilah, Jezebel, and Athaliah are terrible instances of evil influence.

Between the happy cases, the definite and bright colors of good and the extreme and appalling ones, the dark gloomy colors of evil, we have a multitude of indefinite shades, cases varying according to their influence for good or evil. But there can be no doubt as to the fact of influence one way or another. How often we read, his mother's name was so-and-so. No elderly woman can recognize this fact without corresponding concern, surely.

What influence are you exercising, dear sister, in the locality where the Lord has placed you? What is your influence in your home, among other Christians, in your business, if thus engaged? What, particularly, is the effect of your influence on the younger women? It is of this latter I especially wish to speak.

There is sanction in scripture to address in ministry special classes of persons. "The elders which are among you," we read. So also, "Likewise ye younger." In this paper I make bold to address the class described as "The elder women for I recognize the enormous possibilities of their influence, I also appeal to the "younger women," for later on they will have to fill the place of elder women, if the Lord leaves us here. I think I feel the delicacy of my task!

To possess the qualities desirable in an elderly woman, when she becomes one, a young sister must needs begin her training at once. She cannot expect late in life to don moral features as she might change her attire. We are formed by habits of thought or mind. A "pose" is soon detected. What we are gives us influence, not striking an attitude. Young sisters will not be influenced for good by unreality. Hence the start of our training must be made early; for by reason of use are our senses exercised. Our moral muscles will only be developed by degrees and gradually.

First, I would refer to the question of "spirit." This obviously is an important matter, possibly the most important. The Apostle Peter in his epistle speaks of "a meek and quiet spirit," and says that it is of great price in the sight of God. A striking contrast is this spirit to that generally seen in women today, women of the world, I mean. "Assertive and loud" might more aptly describe most, affecting even their voice and manner. Assuming to take a place possible to be filled alone by man, leaving her own valuable and beautiful position, a woman is quickly destroying her truest beauty!

We can scarcely conceive that Mary of Bethany was marked by anything other than "a meek and quiet spirit." Where had she acquired these lovely features? Was it only a feature of womanly grace that led her to remain in the house until called? Scarcely so! She had sat and listened at the feet of Jesus. Who can measure the gain of those blessed moments? Women, I suppose, are characteristically more talkative than men, exceptions but prove the rule. But Mary is marked by sitting and listening. She was listening to One who was meek.

A meek and a quiet spirit is much more powerful in influence than we might suppose. Assertiveness and noise are generally very useless elements and a sign of weakness. And we are expressly told that a meek and quiet spirit is in the sight of God of great price. Happily there are many such women among us today. What a value they are! All, alas, are not so.

As one of the "elder women," do the younger women see this feature in you, dear sister? Are you influencing them by your example in this direction? "A meek and a quiet spirit, which is in the sight of God of great price."

Closely allied to the matter of our spirit is that of speaking. Power for conversation on spiritual matters is much to be valued. It is in no sense a contradiction of the "meek and quiet spirit" to which I have been referring. Indeed, no! Quite the reverse. What respect fills our hearts as we think of Anna. She was one who could speak of Christ. Sometimes it is difficult to continue for long a conversation on these things. Possibly it is because we have nothing to say. There is no abundance of the heart out of which the mouth can speak. Is it because we have not been listening to Christ? Hearing precedes speaking. If we listen the Lord will help us to speak. Are we too busy for that one needful and good part?

Many happy opportunities are given to sisters to speak of Christ without in any way stepping out of their place as women. With widows or maiden sisters who have households, family prayers and the reading of scripture affords one opportunity, as also to wives in the absence of their husbands. Visiting is another opportunity. Dealing with tradesmen is a third. To mothers, what a privilege it is to speak of Christ to their children! What a service a wife can render as she encourages her husband and communes with him on divine matters. It is not at all uncommon for a wife to be more spiritual than her husband. A meek and quiet spirit need not be abandoned, nor her place as a woman and a wife, as she encourages her husband thus. Do not such passages as Judges 1:14, 13:3 and 9, 1 Samuel 1:11, 2 Kings 4:9 teach this principle ?

Seeing this feature in "elder women" would encourage the younger women on similar lines. But to speak we must listen. We cannot teach young Timothys the scriptures unless we know them.

Another matter I would refer to is grace of manner or bearing. This is also closely allied to spirit, as it gives weight to or detracts from our speaking. 1 Timothy 3:11, Titus 2:3-5, 1 Peter 3:5, 6, are passages that speak of this. May I ask my reader to refer to the passages and read them? The manner, deportment and bearing of an elderly sister has a great influence over young ones. Customs and manners catch on, if I may use such an expression, and worldliness of bearing is easily copied. The value of gravity and unworldliness of manner cannot be over-estimated.

How valuable such elder women are! Thank God for those we know, women who can "teach the young women to be sober, to love their husbands, to love their children, to be discreet, chaste, keepers at home, good, obedient to their own husbands, that the word of God be not blasphemed." May God raise up many more such! There may be great activity among certain classes of women, activity it may be even in evangelical or on pastoral lines. But what is the use of this activity if the homes and habits of our young women are not in keeping with the verses I have quoted? A life modeled on the lines of Titus 2 may appear very ordinary to a "modern girl." Such habits may be lightly esteemed. Away with the worthless idea! What power indeed there is in women who love and are subject to their husbands, who love their children, who guide the house with godly order. What weight their words will carry! What influence they wield for good. If we regard our children as "fair to God," if we hold them in trust for Him, how happy the woman's life, how valuable, as day by day she fills out in piety her natural sphere and trains her child for God and discharges her sacred trust!

In this connection another consideration presents itself. Is there not need for spiritual diligence? How apt we all are to become spiritually lazy! What a help it is to young women when they see the elder women marked by distinct spiritual diligence and energy. I do not refer to natural energy. Spiritual energy is what is required, energy which is the fruit of the Holy Spirit; so easy to get occupied with our natural circle, our domestic affairs, the order of the house, the well-being of our children. These are matters surely not to be neglected, but to be taken up in the fear of God. Piety is bringing God into our things. But something more than this is required for spiritual energy. We are to be set for the things of Christ. Are we marked by spiritual energy in taking up the interests of Christ? Do we show energy in following up the ministry, which the Lord gives? Are we energetic in private prayer and in reading scripture? What scope for energy, what need for it if we are to follow the Lord as Caleb did and enter that goodly land! And then energy in service. Who can read Proverbs 31 and not be impressed with the fact that the virtuous woman is marked by an intense and energetic interest in the affairs of her husband and her household, typically, Christ and His own? Do we inquire, "What is to be done?" The Lord has given to each his work. It is for each to see that her own particular work is done. A spiritually energetic and diligent elder woman has immense influence. A mother in Israel is valuable indeed!

My paper is getting long; I must be brief; one word as to adornment. This, as we have seen, is not to be outward, the wearing of gold or costly array. Have some sisters overlooked these instructions of the Apostle Peter? (Chapter 3:3-4) Have the verses been omitted from the Bibles of some of the "elder women"? Have they not read them. We can only charitably suppose that they have been overlooked when we see elder women wearing necklaces and jewelery and donning clothes of indeed costly array! Are we returning to Egypt with its customs? Has Babylon with its goodly garments and gold caught our eyes? Have our women retained their mirrors and not surrendered them to make a "laver"? Or is scripture wrong?

We need not wonder if young sisters are marked by these things when "elder women" lead the way! May I appeal to the elder women? Remember your influence. Every mark of the world is a reproach! Away with your outward adornment, your fashionable clothes! The cross forbids them. Ask yourself why you wear your adornment. Is it for Christ? Are we not followers of a rejected Jesus? Lead, then, the way in piety, in gravity, unworldliness of dress, and be an influence for good. Young sisters are watching you and are being influenced by your manners and course.

And to the younger may I appeal. Let your life be for Christ. Value what He values. If you are to be a power later, and in measure now, you must be separate from the world. Its customs, manners, style and dress are a hindrance in your path and will sap all the vigor from your soul.

"Elder women"! What value they can be! What power there is in a life of devotedness to Christ of uncompromising separation from the world, of spiritual energy. The Lord raise up many such true mothers in Israel!

M.W.Biggs, Enfield, 1931

Excerpt

Ques. What would you say as to the exercise of Rebecca? Does she suggest something in a subjective way that lays hold of the thought of God, and which, in that way, rises above the declension? (deterioration)

JT: Clearly, she is brought in with Sarah, and Rachel, and Leah, as developed out of the generations of Shem and Terah, showing the import of those generations and how cumulative they are, so that we should be instructed as to what we have to do with. Rebecca had the mind of God about the two sons; she loved Jacob. That is, she augmented the fatherly thought, because it is not only the thought of God Himself as Father, but the idea of father in those who are responsible – as you get it with Paul and John and others to whom that title applied. The fatherly thought is often weak amongst the brothers and has to be augmented or supported by the maternal side.

PL: Would that be seen in Deborah, a "mother in Israel", and would Barak represent the weak paternal side?

JT: Exactly, and in Manoah too; you have the maternal qualities in his wife without mentioning her name; the qualities are what is stressed. You have it also in Gideon's mother, who had the right ideal – her sons, as described by the kings of Midian, show that her ideal of manhood went beyond her husband.

J.Taylor, sr. Ministry Vol. 42 p. 476

The Service of Visiting

"Then shall the King say . . . I was sick, and ye visited me. Then shall the righteous answer him, saying, When saw we thee sick and came unto thee?

And the King shall answer and say unto them, Verily I say unto you, Inasmuch as ye have done it unto one of the least of these my brethren, ye have done it unto me."

With these remarkable words the Lord Jesus would stir up the hearts and activities of those who love Him, in relation to the visitation of the sick — both privately and in public institutions.

This is essentially a service of love and sympathy after the pattern of the service of Jesus "who went about doing good." The "compassions of God" were tenderly expressed in His life and were especially displayed when He stood by the bedside of the sick. How familiar He was with suffering, for He was the "man of sorrows and acquainted with grief!" Now He would send forth His willing followers under the impulse of His love to express His compassionate sympathy towards those so greatly in need of Him and of His comfort, ever remembering how frequently He was "moved with compassion."

A vast field of service lies open to both brothers and sisters, for not only in the homes, but in hospitals, infirmaries and many other institutions there are sick ones looking and longing for some one to speak to them of Christ and to point them to God's way of salvation.

The magnitude of the opportunity has been deeply impressed upon every one who has taken up this service. One instance will suffice. A dying woman in the ward of a provincial infirmary greeted the visitor with the words, "Oh! will you tell me something that will give me peace?" The look of intense anxiety and eagerness indicated that the cry, "Come over and help us," once heard by the apostle Paul, is still being heard from the sick and dying around us.

The welcome that is accorded to those who do visit, and the

pathetic appeals for more visits, leave the deep impression that only the very fringe of the field is being explored, and encourages the earnest call for prayer and willing-hearted service in this sphere where "thc harvest truly is great, but the laborers are few; pray ye therefore the Lord of the harvest, that he would send forth laborers into his harvest."

It is possible that some reader of this paper readily acknowledges the need and apprehends the importance and possibilities of this service, but has never considered that the Lord is waiting for his or her reply, "Here am I; send me."

Very frequently such a suggestion brings the answer, "But I am not suited for this character of work." May it be asked, Do you know that you are not fitted for it: are you sure that if you went (timidly it may be) you would not be able to read a few verses, or give a word of comfort with a cheering smile or, better still, pray at the bedside, from a heart moved with compassion, a few simple words that will not only be heard in heaven, but bring blessing and comfort to the sick one?

It has been well said, "The sense of inefficiency does not damp true energy; it only makes one more humble and more reliant on the Lord."

Every one who has embarked on this service has, at some time, been deeply humbled by a sense of incompetence and has often been tempted to leave the task to others more fitted for it, but *is it necessary* to have a "gift" in order to speak to an individual soul of Christ? Is it not rather heart "that is essential? Would not skill be attained by "patient continuance in well doing," and wisdom be gained by experience?

Moreover, "gift" is often given in answer to desire. The Lord loves to work with His servants and to confirm the word. The best way to become efficient is to do the work and to continue to do it.

Many of the Lord's people have a longing to be entrusted with some definite service and yet have not awakened to this sphere of labor, which is at hand and which furnishes such grand opportunities for testimony, experience, enlargement and encouragement.

Some may ask, "But are there open doors, having regard to the increasing stringency of the regulations of public institutions?" There are admittedly many places in which the service may have to be limited to visiting known individuals or where those who visit must be prepared for small things, but there are known to be many such places where there are already open doors and others where by tactful inquiry and by gaining the confidence of those in authority, a wider door may be opened, so that the opportunity of speaking a gospel word in the wards or of distributing books would be given.

The question of cost must inevitably arise. It is certain that it will involve self-sacrifice, some unpleasant experiences, rebuffs and possibly discouragements as well as the expenditure of considerable valuable time and money. Yet it is well worthwhile, for it yields manifold more in this present time and in the world to come life eternal.

Gospel books, tracts and magazines are eagerly received and read again and again by those upon beds of sickness, even by those who might have scorned them when in health. Sorrow, pain and the presence of death are often used of God to open avenues to the heart for the message of the gospel.

While this service is open to all those who love our Lord Jesus Christ in sincerity, it is with an earnest desire that young brothers and sisters will be encouraged to take it up under the Lord's direction and with compassionate hearts, that this appeal is made. First of all it would be for the Lord's sake; then in compassion for those in need, but also because it would yield so much spiritual blessing to their own souls. One who had visited much said, "Visit not so much to do good as to get good and so to be better qualified for doing good."

There is great danger in having no specific work for the Lord on hand, and in the activities indicated there lie such possibilities of development in testimony, sympathy and experience. If the desire is present, do not wait until you feel competent for the service, gain competency by the Lord's gracious help in the work itself !

Be content with a very small beginning. One soul known to you visited in prayerful dependence upon God, may be His way of initiating you into this great service, which awaits young, earnest, devoted and self-sacrificing laborers.

May the Lord stir us all up that this important labor of love may prosper greatly for His own glory.

F.S.Marsh [from — "Words of Grace & Encouragement", vol. 8, pg. 322]

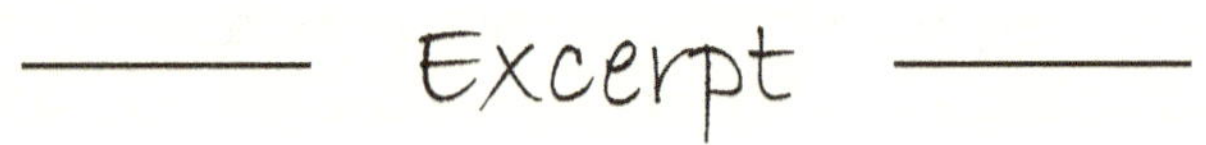

Ques. Was that also the case with the women in Luke 8:3, who "ministered to him of their substance"?

J.T. That is just what we are speaking about. The women had substance and served the Lord with it. Perhaps a sister may say, 'What shall I do then? I am not allowed to speak in the meeting'. But if we really understand that the assembly is a body, we should also know how to make use of the spiritual substance of a sister. For 1 Corinthians 12 the body of Christ is regarded as a living entity. If we had a body which could do nothing more than speak, then we could not turn to account the spiritual substance of our sisters. We must not forget that speech only serves to express what is present and formed in the body. The Lord has ordained that the brothers are to speak in the assembly but they express what is to be found there. The assembly is in a certain sense a vessel in which spiritual power and spiritual abilities are to be found; these only come into evidence and expression in what the brothers say. Thus a spiritual sister who receives a fresh impression from the Lord will tell the brothers about it at home and see to it that a brother gives expression to it in the meeting. Of course, if the sisters think they have no substance, then the assembly is thrown upon the substance of the brothers only.

J.Taylor, sr., Ministry Vol. 77 p. 231

Counsel for Sisters

Our brother spoke of the importance of the sisters' conversation in the home, which is their sphere. A sister can stimulate her husband by asking questions of local and universal assembly interest, and the children who are listening will learn to do the same. If there are visitors in the house, brothers or sisters, she is still in her right sphere in introducing suitable spiritual topics. If she finds her subjects of conversation limited, she would do well to read current ministry extensively, and to make herself acquainted with the latest 'war news', that is, the movements of the testimony world-wide, and thus furnish herself with a store of holy conversation.

The women of this world find a certain pleasure in the discussion of books, newspapers, and literature of various kinds; much more should the Christian woman intelligently read the precious, living ministry which the Lord is giving and thus develop the ability to stimulate and support godly conversation.

The sisters are the unseen, vital organs of the body – the heart and lungs, as it were – and where these are in a healthy state the whole body functions. The brothers are like the hands and feet, the active parts, which are seen. If the body has a high temperature, showing that there is something wrong inwardly, although perhaps nothing can be *seen*, eventually the outward activities of the hands and feet will be impaired.

A word fitly spoken is like apples of gold in baskets of silver (see Proverbs 25:11). The basket of silver would be the body of the believer, silver speaking of redemption. It would be a chaste and wrought piece of silver, fashioned by suffering, containing the precious golden apples – gold being the best – some word bearing the divine impress. Sisters like to see food daintily served; how important the basket is; it makes the apples seem more appetising, especially if a word of exhortation is to be fitly spoken. In all the dispensations there have been women who have stood for the testimony, such as Sarah, Deborah and Jael. And there have been women of all ages. In Rhoda we have a young girl in her teens. Mary, the mother of our Lord, would have been young too. Elizabeth was old, and Anna was very old, all showing that we can enlist and be in the conflict whatever our age.

'Feelings' play a large part in a woman's make-up, but the Lord knows all about our make-up and these feelings and, under the control of the Lord, they can be an asset to the assembly. A sister's instinct can sometimes outstrip a brother's judgment and she may see farther than her husband in choice spiritual feelings. But, on the other hand, her feelings, if uncontrolled, may get the better of her and can make quite a conflagration. Perhaps she has been offended, and her feelings hurt. One has heard such words as, 'It did upset me when I saw the way she looked at me', and so on. It would be well to remember why we are to be silent in the assembly and, as women, to have our head covered, and not take it as a matter of course. It has to do with the fact that Satan at the begimring found an entrance through the woman. God knows that Satan would find an entrance again if the woman were allowed a place of public responsibility. This thought would be wholesome and would keep us humble. As we remember what our possibilities for evil are, perhaps our feelings would not be so offended.

We are not much use in the assembly until we have lost our reputation, or, rather, until we realize that we have no reputation to lose. If we are accused of something that is not true, we can say to ourselves, 'Well, it is not true of me at present, but it might be at any time. I am quite capable of it'. So we remain un-flurried, un-ruffled. God has no use for those who refuse reproach. A sister was known, some time ago, to weep over assembly trouble in a far-distant locality. It seemed an extreme thing to do. Those less spiritual said, 'There is plenty to weep for nearer home'. But she *had* wept for what was nearer home, and had reached out in her affections and interest to assembly troubles at a distance.

She lost her reputation, as it were, and was called 'extreme', but the Lord threw His cloak over her and supported her.

At the end of every dispensation women have shone brightly. The end of the present one is at hand and the Lord would encourage the sisters to more and more devotedness, even to what might appear extreme to the less spiritual.

Sisters love Peter's ministry – his sincere milk of the word – milk, you know, not meat, and what he says as to a meek and quiet spirit. And they love being kind and making garments for the poor and even being the lady bountiful. But the lady bountiful idea only centers round oneself and makes much of self. Making coats and garments ends in death – Dorcas died (Acts 9:37). It was only when Dorcas died to that sort of thing and came to life again that she became part of the assembly on Paul's line. Sisters are inclined to say, 'I can understand Peter's ministry, but I cannot understand Paul's; I will leave that for the brothers'. But they *can* understand Paul. The universal interests of the assembly are for the sisters as well as for the brothers. Sisters have their part in the conflict on the battlefield in the wars of the Lord. They need to be interested in it and to ask and find out what is going on in their midst and in the assembly all over the world. The Lord has His reserves and is preparing them to be called into the front line of the battle, the sisters among them.

If we have those interests before us we shall not feel the dog-flies and gnats, which were among the plagues of Egypt. There were no dog-flies in Goshen, where the Israelites were, suggesting the assembly. The gnats bite only any part of the flesh that is visible. One sister gets a bite from a dog-fly and goes to visit another to get sympathy. She finds that the sister is rubbing her bite very vigorously. They talk so much about their grievances that they only inflame the bites. Indeed, if that piece of flesh is not covered up another piece of flesh may be exposed, and more bites experienced, until in the end that dear sister may die of blood poisoning. There is a nice little service for sisters in 'first-aid'. Perhaps we see a dear sister just bleeding to death spiritually. She is so offended and so hurt by the way she has been treated that her life is ebbing away. What an opportunity for a bandage, a tight, firm bandage! It may be a word in season, one of those precious golden apples, served in the silver basket. A sister who is rendering first-aid, or weaving curtains, or is out on the battlefield, who has the Lord's interests, instead of her own, as her chief object down here, will not feel the bites of the dog-flies or the gnats, nor will she mind if she has no reputation. She will be an asset to the local company, to the whole assembly, and to the Lord.

Percy Lyon

Jottings of household conversation in Melbourne in May 1936

[The above, though not 'ministry' in the usual sense, is printed because it contains valuable counsel, conveyed in the homely manner which characterized our brother—Ed.]

Excerpts

Numbers 27:1-7; Joshua 14:6 -- 15; Judges 1:12 -- 1

So, the book of the Acts corresponds with Joshua in that way, especially reaching in Paul's ministry the heavenly side of the truth which the book of Joshua has particularly in mind. But then we are not in the days of the Acts, we are in the days of 2 Timothy when everything is so difficult, and when there is such public confusion abroad in Christendom which renders things difficult, so that it is a great matter that we should see the setting of Achsah in the book of Judges -- I have deliberately chosen Judges because Judges contemplates what is analogous to our own time, so that none of us might say it was alright in the days of the Acts when the Spirit was operating in the church in the conditions of pristine power and glory that belonged to the church in those days. None of us can say that from the standpoint of the book of Judges, because Judges presents Achsah over against the dark background presented in that book where things were so difficult, I think it is important that this book opens with a young sister manifesting and expressing a desire for the truth. What about the young women here in this gathering now, and in these gatherings for the three days we have been together? Have they got spiritual desires like Achsah? Have they got the desire to go in for divine things, to go in for the blessing, and to get the Spirit, and all the gain of what lies in the Spirit? "Give me also springs of water," verse 15. Let us face the matter tonight, because this book is specially helpful in showing us how the enemy is out to get the young sisters. If he can ensnare them in the world system, all the better from his standpoint, because the young sisters are needed for the carrying on of the testimony as well as the brothers. Deborah, that delightful woman of worth knew that, and she discerned it, and she brought it up in her song; she refers to what the mother of Sisera was saying, and to the strategy in the enemy's camp, and to the counsel of the enemy, and you remember in chapter 5 we get the language that is going on in the enemy's camp. "Have they not found, divided the booty, a damsel, two damsels, to each?" Judges 5:30. The enemy knows what he is after, he is not just after anything, he has specific designs, and especially on the damsels. I would appeal to the young sisters tonight to steel your heart against the artifices of the devil, If he can get you into the world, and to be engrossed with its fashions, so that the most of your time is spent on how you fare publicly in the world and on how you dress, then he has gained a victory over your soul. The divine design is that all your outlook, your exercises, and your concern should center around the blessing connected with the realm of God's selective choice, and your thoughts should center round the gift of God, the outstanding gift of the dispensation, the springs of water, which speak of the Holy Spirit. Reference is made in Numbers 21 to the well which princes dug, which the nobles of the people hollowed out at the word of the lawgiver, with their staves. The gain of the Spirit comes to us as in the type, through the word of the lawgiver. Moses is the great lawgiver. He is a type of our Lord Jesus Christ who has led in the matter of our complete emancipation from the world, typified in Egypt with all its thrall and spell which the enemy would cast over our minds and hearts in relation to it. He has led us forth morally by the Red Sea and broken the power of Satan in our souls, but that is not all. The word of the lawgiver, the digging of the well in Numbers 21 suggests how concerned our blessed Saviour and Deliverer is that we should get the gain of heaven's best, the gift of the Spirit to carry us onwards in the path of the sun-rising, in the path of life in which there is no death, right on and over the Jordan into the realm of God's inheritance, and we may say, our inheritance too.

Beloved young sisters, may there be awakened in your heart's tonight desires in relation to what we have had together, "Give me a blessing," very specific, "Give me a blessing." "What wouldest thou? and she said to him, give me a blessing; for thou hast given me a southern land, give me also springs of water. And Caleb gave her the upper springs and the lower springs." We have been in the southern land these days, we have had that given to us, the rain of heaven has been falling upon us, the favour of God has been shining upon us. God has given us the southern land these days, blessed be His name. And now she says, "Give me springs of water," as if to say that as we return to our localities, we cannot go on in the truth without the power of the Spirit to carry us through, and

I commend the word to the young sisters.

What about the young brothers? Of course, they are not out of this, I am referring to them too. They come into this matter and are essential for the continuance of the testimony, and so we have Othniel here. What a wonderful man Othniel was, and what a link he had with Achsah! It is a great thing, dear young people, when we form right links. There is nothing like bad links to hinder us spiritually. Othniel was the kind of young brother that heaven took account of, and saw that he got a right link in the marital relation. And I would say to you young men, because the marital relation is a normal relation, and a very blessed relation, some of us can speak of it experimentally, and we can thank God for the wives who have been given to us, and who have been a great help and balance to us in the truth -- it is a wonderful thing to get a wife like Achsah, a wife who will help you in the truth. And, young sisters, what a wonderful thing to get a husband like Othniel! A brother who will help you in the truth, too.

I am being very simple about this matter because the matter of marriage has just come into one's mind in proceeding, and it is a very real affair. Some young sisters get so disappointed over this matter that they are prepared to go out of fellowship to get a husband, I would counsel any who might by any chance be thinking along that line. It is disastrous, If your heart is right and if your desires are right, God will provide for you, and you may rest assured of that.

S.McCallum "Spiritual Desires" volume "Spiritual Quality" page 236

Our local meetings have a very precious character, for the body works. Gift would want to be out of sight if it was there, else it might block the whole thing. According to Timothy the sisters are silent, and it is only as the brothers are in the gain of the body that sisters' impressions are realized. There is a need of pauses and of waiting on the Lord, keeping our knowledge in the background, feeling our way for what touch comes in from Christ at that moment. What one receives in his local meeting are his richest impressions and these help him in his wider sphere of service. Paul agonizes in prayer that there might be a state for this -- hearts comforted, knit together in love, etc. Gift is not mentioned in Colossians. When Paul left a local company, he never knew if gift would be there again, for traveling was difficult in those days. So, he would seek to get them growing up to Christ as Head sufficiently for the body to work; and the basic necessity is comfort and being "knit together in love". We need not be troubled if our locality is isolated, for, as set together body-wise, all the treasures of wisdom and knowledge are available to us.

G.R.Cowell "Habitation of God in the Spirit" vol. 50 pg. 63

Aquila and Priscilla

Acts 18:1-3; 1 Corinthians 16:19; Romans 16:3

These scriptures bring before us a husband and wife, mentioned by name, and I wish to say just a word or two as to marriage "in the Lord."

The apostle Paul in writing to the Corinthians refers to what is open to sisters under certain circumstances, as to marriage, and he says, "only in the Lord," as though he would emphasize that as the great essential for Christians. If they contemplate marriage and enter into it, the essential is that it should be in the Lord. I understand that to involve that, in taking up the marriage tie, those concerned are moving practically in the recognition of the Lord Jesus, as subject to Him in their movements, and also that they recognize that there is a sphere here in this world where the Lord's rights are acknowledged and where His interests are, and they have in view that their marriage should stand related to that sphere. This idea of marriage in the Lord is well exemplified in this husband and wife referred to in these and other scriptures.

In the detail of married life we may, with the greatest confidence, face everything that comes upon us, as trusting in God and proving continually the grace of our Lord Jesus Christ; and, if our married life is taken up in relation to God, it affords happiness and blessing which are but little known otherwise. At the same time it is well to bear in mind that – Christ having died, having indeed been cast out of this world, and having gone on high, and the Holy Spirit having come – God is occupied now with what Scripture speaks of as "the spiritual," rather than the natural. "First... that which is natural; and afterward that which is spiritual," I Cor. 15 : 46.

The happiness of our brother and sister will be purest as they hold their married life in relation to the spiritual order of interests, which belongs to them with all God's people here on earth. So, on the only occasion on which we read of the Lord Jesus being present at a marriage, it was allowed that the wine should run out. The Lord was there as gracing the occasion with His presence and approving of it; at the same time He would have them understand from the very outset that, however blessed the marriage link and the joy connected with it as taken up with God, it is not of an abiding character. There is that which is greater and abiding, which is to be known in connection with the saints of God and the interests of God that are cherished in that circle.

So, we find with Aquila and Priscilla that all that is recorded of them in the divine record is connected with their path as identified with what God was doing on the earth at the time. They had come to Corinth, as all Jews had been commanded by the emperor to depart from Rome. No doubt that would cause a good deal of difficulty and concern to both husband and wife, this arbitrary change under such circumstances. It would perhaps involve that they were threatened with the loss of their livelihood; it would involve all the upset of changing their home, and a journey of considerable distance. But whilst the Lord is in no way indifferent to these matters that arise in the practical life of His people, the Spirit of God does not dwell on such details. He would not have such to be uppermost in our minds, but rather the testimony of our Lord, in our homes and in our paths, in our prayers and exercises, in all our movements. As it is so, we shall find that the grace of Christ and the mercy and faithfulness of God will be more than equal to all temporary difficulties or upsets that may arise in the detail of our lives.

Paul... came to Corinth; and found a certain Jew named Aquila... with his wife Priscilla... and came unto them. And because he was of the same craft, he abode with them, and wrought; for by their occupation they were tentmakers," Acts 18:1-3. They had their occupation, but in it they were privileged to have no less a person than the apostle Paul living with them, showing that their house was, in the Lord's sight, worthy to be connected with His name and His interests in this world.

Later we find that they move on to Ephesus, and there they are a great help in their house to Apollos, for we read that "they took him unto them, and expounded unto him the way of God more perfectly," Acts 18:26. It shows what is open to a brother and sister who in singleness of heart cherish the interests of Christ, for they are used to help one that was going to be prominent in the Lord's work.

In Corinthians, written apparently from Ephesus, they were in their second home since being expelled from Rome, and the apostle says, "Aquila and Priscilla salute you much in the Lord." They have that idea of "in the Lord" and they are carrying it right through. They had been at Corinth in their earlier days and knew the brethren there, and in view of the conditions existing there they saluted them "in the Lord," not on merely natural lines, but retaining that idea of "in the Lord and bringing it to bear upon the Corinthians, if so be it might be used to help them in the conditions in which they were. In this connection we read of "the assembly in their house" – a privileged house, indeed, to be so connected with divine interests!

"Salute Prisca and Aquila, my fellow-workmen in Christ Jesus, ...and the assembly at their house," Romans 16:3-5. A commendation that is worth coveting! They had been marked by a whole-hearted devotion to the interests of the Lord Jesus on earth, showing itself in attachment to the apostle Paul and the following up of his teaching, and then "who for my life staked their own neck." At Rome again they are found in this privileged position, that the assembly is in their house. These are great possibilities, that are open to a Christian husband and wife as moving together in the Lord, the possibilities that their house may afford.

On the other hand, we have to watch our houses, as to what emanates from them; for they may become, if we are not preserved in continual self-judgment and dependence upon the Lord, a means of assailing the testimony. In Acts we have another husband and wife – Ananias and Sapphira. This household, alas! had not been conducted in the light. The husband conceived a deception, his wife being privy to it a solemn warning as to houses being corrupted by the husband and wife not being maintained in communion with the Lord. Where, however, the husband and wife conduct their house as truly of one mind in the Lord there is no limit to the privilege and blessing that is open to it.

A.J.Gardiner, Streatham, London, 1937

—— Excerpt ——

"In the Lord" means that the natural will is superseded; that my will is not in it. It is the will of God. The authority of God is vested in the Lord Jesus, and hence marriage "in the Lord' implies that the will of God prevails, and not the natural wills of those entering into this relation.

We have here parents on both sides, true sons and daughters of Abraham, thank God, so that our dear brother and sister are well set out. Both have descended from right families, and the parental feelings to which I have alluded, exist. The wedding feast made by the king for his son, is reflected here; this is seen in what is provided for us here today; but then the thought now is that this parental principle should go down; that it should pass on. It is one of the greatest heritages that we have, the principles we have spoken of properly cherished and exercised in one generation, handed on to the next, all originating in God.

We have the right parents, and our young brother and sister are to cherish the principles in which they have been tutored, and in turn hand them down. It will be exercised in a variety of ways. It enters into the household, into entertainment of the saints, into hospitality generally, and into many other relations and circumstances.

J.Taylor, sr. Ministry Vol. 48 pg. 377

Man and Woman

Deuteronomy 22:5

"There shall not be a man's apparel on a woman, neither shall a man put on a woman's clothing; for whoever doeth so is an abomination to Jehovah thy God". Divine order is ever to be observed, and it is most important to have regard to this in a day when every feature of that order is being so largely set aside. In Christianity the man and the woman each have their distinctive clothing, and are only suitably adorned as they appear in it. The whole tendency of things today is to subvert divine order, but that order is to be maintained in GOd's assembly. Nature itself teaches a woman to be retiring and modest. Her glory is her long hair, which is "given to her in lieu of a veil". Her distinctive glory according to nature suggests what is her true moral glory. Her "clothing" would represent her whole deportment and appearance, not excluding her actual dress. It is to be suitable to the place which she has of expressing in her own person how the assembly is subjected to the Christ.

So Paul, representing the authority of the Lord, says, "Let a woman learn in quietness in all subjection; but I do not suffer a woman to teach nor to exercise authority over man, but to be in quietness", 1 Timothy 2:11, 12. He also says, "Let your women be silent in the assemblies, for it is not permitted to them to speak; but to be in subjection, as the law also says it is a shame for a woman to speak in assembly", 1 Corinthians 14: 34, 35. There might be cases where sisters were more spiritually intelligent than brothers, but they are not to teach. J.N.Darby said that in such cases the saints would be more edified by the observance of divine order than they could possibly be by the superior intelligence of the woman.

I have no doubt that the disordered state of the church is reflected in the uncomely behaviour of women at the present time, one feature of which is the hideous fashion of cutting their hair short. It is a reproach to see women preaching, or putting themselves into prominence; it is a setting aside of their true glory – a putting on of man's apparel.

But then, on the other hand, "neither shall a man put on a woman's clothing". The men are not to retire from the place accorded to them; they are to "pray in every place (that is, not only in the assembly, but at home, or wherever occasion arises), lifting up pious hands, without wrath or reasoning", 1 Timothy 2:8. The public expression of praise or prayer, the setting forth of things in ministry, and the responsibility for order and edification in the assembly, rests with the men, and it is well for all believing men to see that they do not retire from the responsible service of the house of God. It might be as uncomely for a brother to be silent in the assembly as for a sister to speak there. It is well to reflect upon this, and to see to it that we appear in the habiliments, which are suitable.

It is a day in which women are taking a prominent place in public religious activities, but it seems to me that this is a reproach upon the men. If the men had been wearing their proper apparel, and filling up their responsibility according to divine order, there would not have been occasion or room for the women to take the place which they have taken. But to violate divine order in regard to these things is serious; it has the character of "abomination to Jehovah".

C.A.Coates, *Outline of Deuteronomy, pg.282*

...the wife is to be a sister and that marriage is to be in the Lord. The sisterhood of the divine family begins with Terah... that is what Abraham alludes to, the sisterhood whence the wife had to be secured... Then when the actual nuptials take place they must be in the Lord. It is more than family; it refers to fellowship; it refers to the authority of Christ. One might be a Christian, as we say, that is, a believer to a certain point, but be in evil associations. A marriage with such a one could not be in the Lord.

J.Taylor, sr. Ministry vol. 46 pg. 506

The Activities of Sisters

Exodus 1:15-17, 2:1-8, 35:25-29, 38:8

I desire to say a word which may bear in a special way upon our sisters. I have turned, as feeling directed of the Lord, to this book for the purpose of showing how the activities of what is sisterly amongst the saints not only relate to matters of personal and domestic help and blessing, but also contribute in a permanent and substantial way to the service of God.

It is due to our sisters that they are not neglected, for they are under a peculiar obligation in relation to divine things. They are tested, doubtless, in spirit, in the acceptance of the stringent injunctions which preclude from them audible contribution in the public position, but they need to be encouraged to accept in love these injunctions from the Lord, and fill them out with feminine dignity, and in subjection of spirit which in the sight of God is of great price. They are doing this, thank God, and word of encouragement will help them in the support of all that is amongst us of the interests of Christ.

There are some features of sisterly activities in the scriptures we have read. Would that we had in every locality sisters who exercise these qualities! We are faced with circumstances very much akin to those which obtained when Pharaoh issued the edict that the male children should be slaughtered, but through sisterly faithfulness to God the male children were preserved alive. God has seen to it that the names of these two women have gone down in the spiritual history of the saints. They are named Shiphrah and Puah. These women stood out in spiritual brilliance, as their names mean, over against the dark and insidious thrusts of the enemy to impair what was for the service of God.

May we not encourage this in our localities! If sisters cannot participate in preaching or in the service of God in audible thanksgiving, there is remarkable scope opened up to them in this matter of spiritual care, God has endowed women with peculiar ability to enter sympathetically into matters of spiritual travail. I believe there are many of note amongst us who have owed to sisterly care their promotion in spiritual matters. Sisters have entered sympathetically into those early exercises of travail that have marked prominent servants of the Lord. I recall remark made about a sister, who though confined to bed, had watched an honored servant with spiritual care and had prayed for him from the outset. The church of God universally has reaped the value of that bedridden sister.

Now cannot the dear sisters exercise this quality prayerfully in our localities? Are our sisters watching for souls in exercise who come in and out amongst us, as well as the children of the saints who may have early soul-exercise in relation to spiritual matters? Are our sisters alert as strangers come into our gospel meetings, and with feminine grace able in a comely way to get alongside of such and assist them into the enjoyment of what is for them in the thoughts of God? Are they in prayerful spiritual dignity entering into the exercises of souls?

I can recall, in my early exercises amongst the brethren, going into a meeting in the Midlands and an aged sister calling me aside after the meeting and saying, "I have a word from God for you." That is over twenty-five years ago, and that dear sister's word for me has stood me in good stead. "Remember, dear brother," said she, "that you have a place in the affections of Christ which no one but yourself can fill." It was a word from God to my soul, at a moment of great discouragement; it helped me in my spiritual experience to get a gleam of light as to the thoughts of God in sonship. What service the sisters have! Apart from being under the subduing influence of Christ they can work havoc amongst the saints, but what an asset in our localities are the Shiphrahs and Puahs who move in sisterly care for those in early exercise! God made them houses, as if God would help this kind of service permanently amongst His people. That is heaven's estimate of the quiet and unobtrusive activity of two sisters who were concerned about that which was to be for the service of God. This is open to all our sisters, and the Spirit of God would empower them to fill out the place of spiritual midwives in a day when the world is making a bid for our young men and women. I appeal to those who are young to give heed to the spiritual concern of the sisters who would put their arms around you and remind you of the sympathies amongst the saints which are ready to help you into spiritual manhood.

We find in chapter 2 another woman. She is not named here. The name of this woman is held in the chronicles of heaven. "A man of the house of Levi took a daughter of Levi." In the world marriage is becoming a farce, and the tentacles of worldly associations have got hold of many believers. How many have been lost to the testimony through a link with a worldly person! But this man takes a daughter of Levi, and what a daughter she was! What a treasure is a wife who has the interests of Christ at heart! The other two children are not mentioned at this juncture; it is Moses who is recognized as being fair. We should take account of this in Exodus where the woman's part is stressed * what is sisterly and motherly amongst us is being stressed in ministry. Her husband is joined with her in other scriptures, but she stands alone here. If there was ever a day when the maternal influences were needed, it is to-day. We need mothers; we need fathers. There are plenty of teachers. You may have ten thousand teachers but not many fathers, Paul said. We need parental care amongst the brethren. Let us see to it that our desires are on these lines – those of caring for the souls of the saints.

So, this woman has a choice child – fair to God. That is a good start in regard of our offspring. Not thinking of them as to their natural ability, but regarding them in their potentialities as those who will fill a place in the will and service of God. May we as parents hold our children in that light! When he was three months old (she started off well) she took for him an ark of reeds. As the result of the death of Christ there is that available which can be taken up in faith and clothed and made watertight by the activities of maternal care. How many there are who put their children in the ark of reeds and drown them! Unless our sisters – the mothers amongst us, are concerned to plaster the formal rite of baptism with the resin and the pitch, we may as well not baptize our children. It enters into the fiber of our family lives; one would encourage those who are mothers in relation to the little ones committed to them, to see that they are making the rite of baptism a watertight matter. What is the use of baptizing our children if we do not surround them with these personal impressions of Christ? You have to get your resin from Christ. In the activities in your home with the children, see that you are plastering the ark of reeds with resin – what you gather from Christ personally, those early impressions that mothers are able to give to their children freshly each day. They become a barrier in their souls against the floods of worldly influences.

Dear sisters, see to it that you get a supply of resin from Christ. Some of us fathers have to leave home far too early in the morning to permit of a family reading; much is relegated to what the mother can do in this way. Mothers with all the high pressure of modern life must see to it that things are suspended to make room for the resin and the pitch for the children before they go off to school, God honors the exercises of the mothers in caring for them. The simple reading of the word and the committing of the children to God before they go to school, doing it every day, helps to make the ark watertight. The ark of reeds alone would never save anyone; many young ones are being drowned because the parents have been lax about the resin and the pitch.

Dear sisters, hold the children in relation to Christ. Whatever they may give to you in the way of natural affection, however much they may give in the family circle, let it be paramount in the heart of every mother that you are holding the children primarily for Christ and His interests, stopping at nothing to put the barrier of the death of Christ and Christ personally between them and the world, so that they may be proof against its offensive powers.

She puts him in the sedge of the river; not in the main stream. She is not concerned about giving him a place in the world, but chooses for him a sheltered position; a place where, if possible, the child would not be exposed unduly to the influences of the world. We have lost many a Moses and many a Miriam because the parents have said that the children had such a good intellect that they must give them a better education. I know the heart-searchings of this with my own offspring. The children need to be sheltered; let us not have thoughts for advancing them in the world, but let us keep them in the sedge of the river. It is said that the mother of a beloved servant said she would rather he became a stone cracker on the road and happy with the Lord than to get the highest position in the land. We do well to comfort ourselves with the fact that divine providence will see that they get through safely. So, she puts him in the sedge by the bank of the river. Oh! the heart-pangs when the children first face the world in having to go to school! If we have not put them into the ark of bulrushes safely covered with the resin and the pitch, we may lose them. Let us see to it that they are safely housed in the right environment in the meaning of household baptism before going to school! She puts him there and retires. I have no doubt Jochebed had her hands full (Aaron would be perhaps three years old and Miriam not much older), but she made room for this important matter.

Miriam could not have been very old, yet it says to her credit that she stood afar off to watch. When later the entry is made in the chronological register it is said, "Aaron and Moses and Miriam their sister." It is a grand thing to have a sister that is prepared to watch to see how the young ones are getting on. Think of that being done by a small girl! She has the answer for the moment. She sees the influence which the daughter of Pharaoh would have, and without any injunction – she would not have been able to give you chapter and verse for what she did – in sisterly love and devotion she says, "Shall I go and call thee a wet-nurse of the Hebrew women." Let us see to it that there are spiritual nurses in our localities; those who are able to nurse with personal spiritual substance the youth that is amongst us. I believe, in this connection, that motherly contribution in a private and secret way forms the great bulwark to what may come out in public ministry. If there is not that ability to nurse the babes in Christ, the most eloquent speaking publicly will be of little avail. If you are not in a state to nurse them yourselves, then find someone who con do so as Miriam did. Here is a work for sisters, and brothers too, as Paul says to the Thessalonian babes in Christ, "but have been gentle in the midst of you, as a nurse would cherish her own children," 1 Thessalonians 2:7.

So Jochebed nursed the child with the knowledge that presently she was going to part with him, and that she had to leave him to the tender mercies of the court of Pharaoh. Some of our sisters may have sons and daughters like this and they have nursed them in relation to the interests of Christ, but the world has claimed them. Jochebed had to wait for forty years for Moses. Do not lose heart, dear sisters; what you have sought to sow in maternal love in the children which God has given you, in His own time He will bring to fruition. Go on in the faith of this and cling to God in the matter. Childhood is soon gone, and the world makes a claim on our families, but if we have sown the seed we can count upon God to bring it to fruition. So, the activities of Jochebed in this beautiful section result in bringing to light a man of God without compare. Moses is the product of maternal affection, and I believe men of God are produced amongst us as our sisters adapt themselves with feminine ability to give them that which builds them up. Paul refers to this quality regarding the mother and grandmother of Timothy a man of God in the New Testament.

Now in chapters 25 to 31, God is speaking to Moses on the mount, and He outlines the tabernacle system objectively. There is the idea in all its perfection, but what is the use of having just the light of things if they are not filled out? In this connection the exercises of the women play a most important part. So, we read in chapter 35 what the sisters are bringing in the way of substantial contribution. Every woman who was wise-hearted spun with her hands and brought what she had spun, the blue and the purple and the scarlet and the byssus and then the goats' hair. What are we bringing into our localities? If we are not watchful, we may be bringing in the latest tit-bits of gossip which may upset the harmony and disturb the unity of the saints. But think of sisters being able to bring in what is substantial in the way of blue. A heavenly influence; a heavenly walk; a heavenly color marking the sisters as they move in their respective localities, Think, of them being able to bring in the purple; not only the idea of what is royal and dignified, but readiness to suffer for it. It is said of Jesus in the gospel by John that He went forth wearing a purple robe, and a crown of thorns. He went forth wearing it; bearing the ignominy and scorn of men. Think of sisters entering into that; the Mary's who stood by the cross of Jesus stood out in their distinctiveness as sharing in the public sufferings of Christ. Do we know anything about the purple? Some of our sisters have suffered through the trade union question; they have suffered in relation to their hair. I have heard of sisters who have lost their jobs because they would not have their hair cut and brought into the latest fashion. Are you prepared to suffer, to hold your hair because of the divine injunction? There is royal womanhood according to God in Esther in her preparedness to obey and suffer – Esther 4:15-16. Are you in it, holding yourself as a vessel for bringing the purple into the public position? Think of how the young girls can contribute to the purple as it stands in its own beauty, bringing it in amongst the people of God. The Beloved says in the Sons of Songs, "I have come into my garden; I have gathered my myrrh with my spice" – not what He brings but what He finds in the saints; the readiness to suffer. When young ones come in on Lord's day to break bread, and they have been reproached for Christ's sake during the week, they come in with the purple as they sit down at the Supper – a heavenly glow and color about them. The scarlet is that which would mark them off as distinctive; not as wearing puritanical dresses, but the way the sisters conduct themselves, their sobriety, all having a dignity and comeliness which is fit for the presence of God.

Then the fine twined linen, the byssus. How it comes down in its application to the simple matters of life! The matter of righteousness in all our activities enters into the smallest details of our lives, and forms a background and basis for all that we bring in to the collective position. Sisters carrying on with all this dignity and charm proper to them provide the basis of that in which God can dwell inside in the curtains. Their byssus may be included in the outside hangings which enclosed the outer court. What weakness there is in the public position because of unrighteousness and lawlessness of women in Christendom! We see something of it. The hangings were five cubits high everywhere, as if to suggest the standard of righteousness maintained publicly in testimony.

Then the goats' hair. A difficult task they must have had spinning goats' hair by hand; yet this is accredited to the women. They are the persons who contribute to this tent which goes over the inner curtains of the tabernacle. Think of the ability of sisters to keep themselves apart from the filthy conversation that is marking many women today, and being able to weave – not just an idea – but to form a covering tent for those beautiful curtains. I believe this is what we need to encourage our sisters in. It is so easy to get caught in the current of the day, but as having the divine dwelling in mind let us take on the idea of weaving the goats' hair, thus making conditions of protective separation.

Now the final word. The laver is a permanent monument in the tabernacle system to the devotedness of godly women, and the Spirit of God is careful to credit them with it. It is said that the women crowded before the entrance of the tent of meeting. What a good word that is! One thinks of how heaven takes account of sisters who are prepared to make domestic sacrifice to be at a meeting like this; it is noted in heaven. Your interest in the truth and in the things of God is marked down in the chronicles of heaven. There is another solemn reference to sisters who crowded the entrance in the days of Eli: there they contributed to the faithlessness of the priesthood with Hophni and Phinehas.

They held not themselves in holy chastity in relation to the things of God. May that be a word of warning to us, alongside of the encouragement! But here in this setting it says, "he made the laver of copper and its stand of copper of the mirrors of the women who crowded before the entrance of the tent of meeting." Think of sisters being prepared to part with their looking-glasses that they might contribute to the service of God in purity; this matter of maintaining purity in the priesthood and doing so by sisterly sacrifice stands perpetually as a monument to the devotion of sisters. The spiritual and priestly state of our gatherings is largely regulated by the ability of the sisters to supply the laver idea. What pure and holy freshness it affords!

Well, dear sisters, you see where it leads. Your devotion, your sacrifice for Christ, your being prepared to part with the nearest thing to your heart, contribute to that which maintains the priesthood in freshness and cleanliness. This is something you can do in your own locality, in helping the priests to keep their hands and feet clean. May our sisters be encouraged in all these features of the service, seeing where it leads and what God gets out of it, to devote themselves more to it while there is opportunity for sisterly service!

J.Darton, Newcastle-upon-Tyne, 1950
From -- "Words of Grace and Encouragement" vol. 26

"The Lord gives the word, great the host of the publishers", Psalm 68:11. Mr. Darby points out that the word publishers there is a feminine one. Mr. Stoney used to refer to the sisters as retrievers going after the wounded.

J.Taylor, sr. Ministry vol. 64 p. 341

How beautiful it is to see, as we sit together in our meetings for prayer, that brothers and sisters alike can retain in their hearts the spiritual utterances of the priests of God -- that is the idea -- so that there is a sustained odour for God, not only in the prayer meeting but continually.

J.Taylor, sr., Ministry Vol. 39 p. 482

Holy Men and Women

Psalm 90:1-2, 1 Timothy 6:11-16, 2 Timothy 3:16-17, 1 Peter 3:3-6, Judges 4:4-5

Having in mind that the assembly is composed of brothers and sisters, men and women, I wish, by the Lord's help, to speak of holy men of God, and of holy women who trust in God. Scripture speaks of both. Peter in his second epistle, tells us that "the prophecy came not in old time by the will of man, but holy men of God spoke as they were moved by the Holy Spirit," 2 Peter 1:21. In his first epistle, in the passage read, he speaks of holy women who trusted in God. In holy men of God, and holy women who trust in God, we have the constituents in moral power of the assembly. As the days become increasingly difficult, and the testimony nears its end, there is an urgent call for such men and women. What is important in the testimony is the truth of God and the rights of God. We are living in days when the power and will of man, energized by Satan, have risen to great heights – the object being to destroy, if possible, from this earth, all that stands for the rights of God and His truth. That calls for men of God and holy women who trust in God.

Women do not stand out publicly in the testimony, though they have their part in it. Their part is rather to provide subjective conditions as a support for it. They form the counterpart of the "men of God." They have confidence in God, which calls down divine support, so that the testimony can go through. Connected with the thought of the men is the ability to stand out as representing God, but the women set out the idea of the subjective conditions, which are necessary for the maintenance of the testimony to the end.

Both ideas are completely set out in the Lord Himself. Did ever anyone maintain the truth of God so perfectly and so blessedly as Jesus? On the other hand, no one was ever marked by such complete dependence and confidence in God as He was, so that He is heard saying, "I was cast upon thee from the womb: thou art my God from my mother's belly;" Psalm 22:10. From the very outset this feature of dependence on God, and confidence in God, characterized Him, and formed the moral basis of the maintenance of the truth of God, right through to the end. Indeed, it became a matter of taunt from his enemies on the cross. They said, He trusted in God; let him deliver him now (Matthew 27:43) That was taken account of by His enemies. Then came the moment of all moments when He was actually forsaken of God, and yet He trusted God right through, and was heard "from the horns of the unicorns," Psalm 22:21.

Moses comes before us as one of the outstanding men of God. Psalm 90 is a "Prayer of Moses the man of God." The idea of a man of God is not limited to the elder brothers, for Timothy was a young brother, and Paul addresses him as a man of God, 1 Timothy 6:11. Moses was a man of prayer, and what was in his soul comes to light in this prayer. He says, "Lord, thou hast been our dwelling place in all generations," Psalm 90:1. He found his dwelling place in God, and thus was not moved by what men said or thought or did. And then, as expressing the sense he had of the greatness of God he says: "Before the mountains were brought forth, or ever thou hadst formed the earth and the world, even from everlasting to everlasting, thou art God." I believe that lies at the root of the constitution of a man of God – he has God before him and not men. The Psalm goes on to speak of the mortality of man, for man is but mortal. When Cain slew Abel – the first man who stood for the rights of God, God gave another son in place of Abel, and his name was called Seth, which means "appointed." God will see to it that there is an appointed seed to carry on the testimony. Then it says, "to Seth... was born a son; and he called his name Enos," which means frail, mortal man, showing that the testimony is to be carried on by men who are mortal and can thus be put to death, but it adds "then began men to call upon the name of the Lord," Genesis 4:26. Their resource was in the name of the Lord.

Moses was fully developed on that line, for he says, "Lord, thou hast been our dwelling place in all generations," and "from everlasting to everlasting, thou art God." As he proceeds, he takes account of the discipline of God, and prays, "So teach us to number our days." He recognizes that life at best is but brief, so that this man of God would impress us with the importance of our days. Abraham died full of days, as also did Isaac. David, Job and Jehoiada, as though every day, or at any rate a large number of the days, of their lives had been such as God could take account of with pleasure. Moses recognizes the brevity of human life, and, too, the urgency of the testimony, and so he says, "So teach us to number our days, that we may acquire a wise heart," Psalm 90:12. Paul had in mind that Timothy, as having already given evidence of the features of a man of God, should be preserved. If Satan sees anyone who is set for the things of God, he will do his utmost to ensnare him or turn him aside in some way or other. So, Paul takes account of that. He had been speaking of the danger of ambition, and then he says: "But thou, O man of God, flee these things." Piety with contentment is great gain. In regard of this life it is the great prescription for a happy and successful life, He continues, "and pursue righteousness, piety, faith, love, endurance, meekness of spirit."

Righteousness is what is right in the sight of God in actual practice. We must not deflect from it, to the right hand or the left. It must be the governing principle of our life. In Proverbs, which has in mind that we should be preserved for God in a world of evil, Wisdom says, "I lead in the way of righteousness, in the midst of the paths of judgment;" Proverbs 8:20. Piety preserves us from ambition and from discontent. It is bringing God into every matter of our life here. And then faith — that is more than confidence in God. Faith means that We are governed by the light of unseen things. We have the great privilege of stepping into the eleventh chapter of Hebrews and continuing that path – the path that commenced with Abel and which will continue till faith gives place to sight.

Then there are *love, endurance,* and *meekness of spirit.* The man who was king in Jeshurun and who led out perhaps two million people – the man who could stand up and maintain the rights of God in a crisis at the time of the idolatry in respect of the golden calf – he was the meekest man in all the earth. One has sometimes wondered how it was that Moses acquired his meekness. I have thought of God showing Moses the pattern of the tabernacle. I have no doubt that God would explain to Moses what it *typified.* How God would delight to speak to Moses of *Him whom the ark typified* and from whom the whole system was to take character — so different from any other man! All that is going to subsist before God is to take character from Him who could say, "I am meek and lowly in heart," Matthew 11:29. I can understand how Moses would become imbued with meekness of spirit!

On one occasion the spirit of Moses was provoked and he spoke unadvisedly with his lips, and for one failure on his part he was denied entrance to the land. It might seem to us arbitrary on God's part, but Moses had failed to hallow God. He was here in this world as representing God, and he had failed to hallow the God he represented.

Timothy is charged in the sight of God who quickens all things and before Christ Jesus – and then the apostle speaks of His appearing, "Which in his times he shall shew, who is the blessed and only Potentate, the King of kings and Lord of lords," 1 Timothy 6:14-15. The Father knows the time; it is in His power. It is to be shown by Him who is King of kings and Lord of lords – which is the sense Paul had of God. He was shortly to appear before the great Roman emperor, but Paul, in his soul, was in the presence of God.

In this first epistle we have what the man of God is to follow if he is to be preserved, and in the second we have his equipment – and that is in the Scriptures. "All scripture is given by inspiration of God, and is profitable for doctrine, for reproof, for correction, for instruction in righteousness: that the man of God may be perfect, thoroughly furnished unto all good works," 2 Timothy 3:16-17. He is to be completely equipped, and complete in his qualifications, as making full use of the Scriptures. It necessitates that we know them, that is, all Scripture. We cannot afford to not accept a single one of the books of the Scriptures. They afford a remarkable armory, and as we acquaint ourselves with them, the Holy Spirit can bring them to our minds to meet any emergency as it arises. There is not a single thing that can arise in the history of the testimony that is not provided for in the Scriptures, and thus the man of God is to be fully fitted to every good work.

"Holy women who trust in God," speak of another aspect of the testimony. The apostle Peter, recognizing the tendency that certain things have to appeal to women, urges upon the sisters to take account of how things are valued in the sight of God. The man of God walks before God, and Peter urges sisters to walk before God and to take account of things as God values them. "Let it be the hidden man of the heart, in that which is not corruptible, even the ornament of a meek and quiet spirit, which is in the sight of God of great price." It is a question of divine valuation, different from that which is current amongst men, and exercising ourselves to be in the sight of God.

There is not only this adornment, but there is this question of trusting in God. He brings forward Sarah, going back all those generations to remind us of one who is the mother of all true believers. She is to be spiritually regarded by sisters as their mother, as Abraham is the father of the faithful. The feature she brings forward is that of complete subjection. She called her husband "lord." The Spirit of God brings that forward as a feature which is particularly pleasing to God. It is not suggesting that sisters by word of mouth should call their husbands "lord." Sarah is not said to have addressed him as such, but in speaking to herself she said, "After I am waxed old shall I have pleasure, my lord being old also," Genesis 18:12. It was not a moment when she was specially in spiritual power, yet, what she is characteristically comes to light. This feature of subjection, which is rapidly being lost in the world, is a feature of great delight to God, and it is urgent in view of the trend of things in this world, that it should be maintained in its true dignity and value amongst the saints. It is a characteristic feature of the assembly herself – she is subject to Christ. The brothers are to set forth the idea of intelligence in the mind of God, whilst the sisters are there to set out the feature of subjection. The complete combination of these two features is to be seen in the assembly. These two things are brought together in 1 Corinthians 14, and all are to be marked by subjection. The spirits of the prophets are to be subject to the prophets. If we would have a true view of the value of subjection, we have only to remind ourselves that in the eternal day the Son Himself will be "placed in subjection to him who put all things in subjection to him, that God may be all in all," 1 Corinthians 15:28. The Son retains this position of subjection eternally in order that all may be held in relation to the blessed God in the light in which He is revealed, so that He may be all in all for evermore.

Subjection is morally glorious – it is the principle on which God recovers and holds everything for Himself, and so one would urge on the sisters that they should take up this idea of "holy women who trust in God." It will show itself in their spirit, and in the true feature of subjection characterizing them in everything, and will call forth divine support for the glorious testimony to which we are committed.

It is of the greatest importance that we should be in the truth of the assembly, and, as it is composed of men and women, that these things should have their place with us. Brothers should be concerned to be men of God, and sisters to be holy women who trust in God. There cannot be, in the assembly, any more spiritual power than that which is found in those who compose it.

A.J.Gardiner, Sligo, 1940

Excerpt

Sisters do not speak in the meetings -- they are obliged to keep silent; but that does not mean that they have not an influence, but the very opposite. They have a profound influence if they are spiritual; God provides for us in this way.

J.Taylor, sr., Ministry Vol. 33 p.36

The Service of Sisters

Exodus 2:1-10, 25:20-29, Esther 4:9-17, John 19:25-27

Much has been said about the brotherly spirit in the assembly, but something might be said about the sisterly spirit. The brotherly spirit is for the support of the house of God, but the sisterly spirit is equally necessary. The great product of the Epistle to the Romans is a sister – Phoebe. Paul says of her in the beautiful letter of commendation which she carried, "Receive her in the Lord, as becometh saints ... for she hath been a succourer of many, and of myself also." (Romans 16:2) This suggests that letters of commendation should not be cold, formal communications – passports to break bread – but as establishing living links between saints in various places. With this in view one would hardly wait till Lord's day morning to present one's letter of commendation, but would seek out the saints during the week, if possible, for it is to their love and fellowship we are commended, and in the breaking of bread.

The passages read present the thought of a sister in Scripture. Miriam is the first true sister mentioned. Dinah was not a true sister; she left the family circle and "Went out to see the daughters of the land." Her surrender of family interests led to her defilement. (Genesis 34:1) The family interests should prevent idle curiosity. In Exodus 2 we have presented three aspects of the care, which should be shown by a sister:

(1) The maternal spirit as seen in the mother of Moses.

(2) The sisterly spirit as displayed in Miriam.

(3) The nursing spirit as shewn by Moses' mother.

The *maternal* spirit in a meeting protects the young saints who have been received into fellowship. The sisterly spirit watches over the divine interest and cherishes the testimony. The nursing spirit is important, too, for the nurse is concerned about the food a child takes, the clothing it wears, and the atmosphere it breathes. How all these elements were happily blended in the Apostle Paul as writing to the Thessalonians he says, “We were gentle among you, even as a nurse cherisheth her children.” (1 Thessalonians 2:7) How jealously he guarded and cared for the young converts! It is the kind of spirit that should mark both brothers and sisters.

The maternal spirit sees the infinite possibilities that lie in the young as being “fair to God.” Stephen says, “Moses ... was exceedingly lovely.” (Acts 7:20, Darby Trans.) The elect lady in the second Epistle of John would be jealous that the young should be preserved for God apart from evil influences; she would shut her door on all who brought not sound doctrine. So, too, the wise woman in Proverbs 31; the result is that “her children rise up, and call her blessed.” (verse 28)

Then the *sisterly* spirit of Miriam might suggest how the link was preserved in the line of the testimony – looking backward to Noah’s ark and forward to the ark of the testimony; that there were immense possibilities in that weeping babe lying in the ark of bulrushes. So she watches over him to see what would happen to him. The time would come when the face of that little babe would shine with all the radiancy and glory of the Covenant. (See Exodus 34:29-35) In this way ought there not to be real desire with us to perceive in the youngest saint some distinctive feature of Christ and to foster it? The little babe that Miriam’s sisterly spirit protected became the greatest saint in the Old Testament. The protective spirit should mark a sister.

Then the *nursing* spirit is exercised under the impulsive power of love. In Exodus we see that the mother becomes the nurse. A mother’s love is a priceless possession; Solomon cherished it. (Proverbs 4:3) So the nursing spirit in a meeting would secure an atmosphere of love. There must be something strangely wrong in a meeting where love is not in evidence. Enquiries as to the “right company” would be solved for many anxious souls if saints have “fervent love” amongst themselves. The Lord Jesus is found in the circle where He is loved. In Matthew we have the expression, “the young child with his mother.” (chapter 2) Thus we can see that the sisters have an equal share in the testimony. It is open to both sisters and brothers to give their color and character to the meeting.

It is interesting to see that Moses' parents did not give him a name. Parents should not seek to give them a name in this world, but a name for God's world. When speaking of the education of children J.N.Darby said, that if he had children he would as soon see them breaking stones as anything else, if he could secure for them the gospel of the grace of God.

In the building of the tabernacle (Exodus 35) two classes of people are mentioned: the willing- hearted and the wise-hearted. The women are referred to as wise-hearted. The contributions of the men typify the service of the brothers in the house of God in the ministry, which is given to them. The sisters can engage in visiting, and in those good works, which bind the saints together. The men in Exodus furnished the material, and the spinning was the work of the women. There should be individual and collective exercise to produce a yield for God. (verses 27, 28)

The offering of the rulers was priestly in character. There are rulers in the house of God — special vessels to whom the Word of God is committed. We ought to bow to sovereignty in regard of such and sympathetically support them. Deborah and Barak sang, "My heart is toward the governors of Israel. (Judges 5:9)

One thing was essential with the men; whatever else they gave they were to give gold. (Exodus 35:22) The Women sacrificed their own beauty and interests to those for the tabernacle; even the laver was made of copper "of the mirrors of the crowds of women." (Exodus 38:8 Darby Translation) They spun materials of various colors.

Blue speaks of what is heavenly. We should be exercised to have a contribution such as this. Mary Magdalene had genuine affection for Christ, and how large a contribution of blue is suggested in the message she carried to the assembly. (John 20:17) She was homeless on earth without Christ, and to her orphaned spirit is revealed the precious knowledge of the new heavenly position and relationships.

The *purple* represents the imperial rights of Christ. Lydia was a sister who associated herself with those who were suffering for Christ. She was not ashamed of this association. She cherished in her heart the imperial rights of Christ. (Acts 16) The Corinthians were reigning as kings, but it was too soon (1 Corinthians 4:8-9), for the present is a suffering period. The saints do not wear the purple today; they cherish it in their hearts in view of its imminent display in Christ. "He alone is worthy o'er all to reign."

The *scarlet* might rather typify the glories of Christ as God's Anointed. The true glory of man is seen in Christ. Saul clothed the daughters of Israel in scarlet, but he was passed over by God to make room for a man after God's own heart. It is that Man, Christ morally, that is to be perpetuated amongst the saints. The wise woman in Proverbs 31:21 clothes her household with scarlet so that they are not afraid of winter.

The *fine linen* is a priestly garment, that which is suitable to the house of God. Hannah brought a linen garment every year to Samuel in the temple. The coat would need to be bigger each year. Thus the sisterly spirit would discern growth in the young saints, and suitably clothe them, taking a spiritual estimate of each and providing garments neither too large nor too small. An example of one who spun goats' hair is seen in the elect lady in the second Epistle of John; she shut her door against the evil-doers and against unsound doctrine. The sisterly spirit would keep out all appearance of evil. Then in

Luke 8 there are sisters who minister to Jesus of their substance, a privilege open to many today. In the passage read in Esther a great crisis had come into the testimony, and the danger was that all the Jews would be destroyed. With what lowly grace Esther lays aside all her queenly dignity and proves her worth as a sister. She would stake all to secure the salvation of her kinsman, and identify herself with them in the fullest measure. In principle she is prepared to die for the people; she says, "If I perish, I perish." Does not the testimony increasingly call for devotedness of heart and mind so that all our interests are held subservient to its demand upon us?

Esther was prepared to sacrifice her dignity as a queen; and her sisterly love for the saints enabled her to do this. No doubt her education had to do with this. She had six months with oil of myrrh, which speaks of suffering and surrender, but this is followed by six months with spices – the fragrance of Christ which we enjoy in the power of the Spirit. The same spirit is shown by Aquila and Priscilla, who laid down their own neck for Paul. The word "neck" is in the singular in the Darby Translation, for under the gracious influence of headship; one motive will influence man and wife – not separate motives – In the interests of Christ. There should be no reserve in what we do for the saints, but spirituality is needed. We cannot maintain silence indefinitely. We are "not to be ashamed of the testimony," nor of the reproach. The right spirit, however, is needed to enter the ranks. "Be strong in the grace which is in Christ Jesus." (2 Timothy 2:1)

In John 19 we have the public position. When the disciples forsook the Lord and fled, it was the women who identified themselves with Him at the time of His supreme suffering. They proved here to be the stronger instead of the weaker vessels. The Lord's mother represents His interests (John 19:25), and the Lord committed her to John who had a home. He is the only disciple said to have a home. John in his precious ministry would provide a home for all the saints, but as he is nameless here – "the disciple whom Jesus loved" – it suggests room for any who care to be charged with the interests of Christ. He will commit them to affection. Mary the wife of Cleopas may have some reference to Christ entering into His glory. (See Luke 23:18-26) Mary of Magdala was the one out of whom seven devils were cast, and she thus stands as a monument of the sovereignty of divine mercy, for nothing else caused her to identify herself with Christ. Our public position today is as standing around the cross; we are not ashamed of that position. Our inside private sphere is where all that is of Christ and for God is being nourished and cherished in view of immediate display. May these things characterize one and all

H.F.Nunnerley, from – "Words of Grace and Comfort," volume 2

The Sister

Marked off from all who on that train were trav'lling,
Clearly distinctive in the crowd and press,
Her presence indefinable and hallowed,
Witness to heavenly grace and pureness.

Untrammelled by the mad extremes of fashion
And free of vanity and worldly craze,
Unsought, a condemnation of the world,
Rebuking, silently, its bent and ways.

Bringing to notice that quiet sobriety
That checks the giddy worldling on his way,
Disclosing solid worth and quiet contentment
Holds forth the light of Christ's soon-coming day.

A station neared, she rose to leave the carriage,
And eyes looked up; sure, some had been impressed,
And envied her deliverance from worldly aim,
Sighed for such peace of mind and quiet rest.

She left the coach, left also an impression.
Fast on its journey rocked the noisy train,
Yet still her presence lingered in the carriage,
The vision stayed—and went—and came again.

Such is the power, which quietly bears witness
That the believer knows another world,
Cherishes deep another hope and object,
Raises a banner, holds it up unfurled.

See how the world its emptiness discloses?
Compare her, worldling, with thy hollow choice,
Great angels marvel at such piety,
Behold God's faultless order and rejoice.

(Based on an actual experience)
N.T.Meek, Malvern, England

The Place of Women

Some poor women – to whom devotedness often gives, on God's part, more courage than to men in their more responsible and busy position – were standing near the cross, beholding what was done to Him they loved.

The part that women take in all this history is very instructive, especially to them. The activity of public service, that which may be called "work," belongs naturally to men (all that appertains to what is generally termed ministry), although women share a very precious activity in private. But there is another side of Christian life which is particularly theirs; and that is personal and loving devotedness to Christ. It is a woman who anointed the Lord while the disciples murmured; women who were at the cross, when all except John had forsaken Him; women who came to the sepulcher, and who were sent to announce the truth to the apostles who had gone, after all, to their own home; women who ministered to the Lord's need. And, indeed, this goes farther.

Devotedness in service is perhaps the part of man; but the instinct of affection, that which enters more intimately into Christ's position, and is thus more immediately in connection with His sentiments, in closer communion with the sufferings of His heart – this is the part of woman: assuredly a happy part. The activity of service for Christ puts man a little out of this position, at least if the Christian is not watchful. Everything has, however, its place. I speak of that which is characteristic; for there are women who have served much, and men who have felt much.

Note also here, what I believe I have remarked, that this clinging of heart to Jesus is the position where the communications of true knowledge are received. The first full gospel is announced to the poor woman that was a sinner who washed His feet, the embalming for His death to Mary, our highest position to Mary Magdalene, the communion Peter desired to John who was in His bosom. And here the women have a large share.

J.N.Darby, Synopsis of the Bible, Vol. 3, p. 191

Then in verse 17 he begins to speak of the order of the Lord's supper as actually celebrated, and the apostle condemns what they were doing. It is quite obvious that the thought of headship should precede this instruction, and so he says, "I wish you to know that the Christ is the head of every man, but woman's head is the man, and the Christ's head God. Every man praying or prophesying, having anything on his head, puts his head to shame. But every woman praying or prophesying with her head uncovered puts her own head to shame; for it is one and the same as a shaved woman. For if a woman be not covered, let her hair also be cut off. But if it be shameful to a woman to have her hair cut off or to be shaved, let her be covered. For man indeed ought not to have his head covered, being God's image and glory; but woman is man's glory. For man is not of woman, but woman of man. For also man was not created for the sake of the woman, but woman for the sake of the man. Therefore ought the woman to have authority on her head, on account of the angels". Verse 10 is one which we should especially notice; there is to be with the woman a token of the authority under which she stands, that is, the authority that is over her. She is to recognise that there is authority over her, and that there is authority over the man too, and that authority is Christ, and even over Christ is God. So that the order is from God to Christ, from Christ to the man, and the man to the woman, and verse 10 is to bring the thing home to the woman, so that she is to be covered in the recognition of the authority under which she stands.

QUES. Would that mean that the apostle approaches the subject of order in the assembly by way of showing that there is order in the universe of God? Has that to do with the universe?

J.T. I would think so. You see from God to Christ and from Christ to man; the word used for man means man as distinct from woman. Therefore the authority is from God to Christ, and from Christ to man, and from man to woman, and then in this instruction we are told that nature should teach us, so that universal authority, I would say, or ornamentation if we may use that word, is in mind. The ornamentation implied in the order of God from Himself down to Christ, from Christ down to the man and from the man down to the woman, is something that we have to ponder over, and see what is meant by it. Why should what is the mere physical action of the woman covering her head, or the man not covering his head, why should these things be mentioned? Surely there must be a very good reason for them to be mentioned and especially in view of the fact that the Lord's supper is just immediately to be celebrated in the chapter.

QUES. Why are the angels brought in here. What relation are they to the

Supper?

J.T. They are creatures, one of the great families of God, and their intelligence is remarkable, their power is remarkable, both these things are alluded to. You see for instance in the case of Manoah, the husband of the woman to whom the Angel appeared, how intelligent the Angel was, and how he acted as God really before Manoah, and his wife, and then how his wife is instructed as to the child that she is to have and how he is to be brought up in the light of power, in the light of his mother and father.

QUES. Have these angels maintained subjection in the presence of insubjection around? They left not their first estate; they are referred to as holy angels.

J.T. There is a family that left not their first estate, and they are viewed as obedient, and are called elect angels. The apostle Paul charged Timothy in the presence of the elect angels, showing how intelligent and important they are in the presence of God.

QUES. Would it be correct to connect the thought of "the head of Christ is God" with the Son being placed in subjection in chapter 15?

J.T. I think that is quite right. The Son shall be in subjection, we are told.

QUES. Would you say that the angels all know that the saints are much beloved? The one that spoke to Daniel said, "O ... man greatly beloved", Daniel 10:11.

J.T. They are conversant with what is current in heaven, and with what is current on earth, too, because they are sent out to minister on account of those who shall be heirs of salvation; they are all sent out for that.

REM. To reflect heaven's interest providentially in the care they exercise.

J.T. Very good; that is very largely how they act, and they are serviceable to God in His providences.

QUES. Is this acknowledgment of the authority under which the woman stands called for only in the assembly?

J.T. I would say at all times. I do not mean when she is sleeping or resting or the like, but where she is functioning in any capacity that a woman should function in. That is what I understand.

QUES. Praying in the home, would she be covered?

J.T. Quite so. It is to bring in the order of God. We may say, Why should it be? Well, God says so and that ought to be enough for every subject heart. If we bow to Scripture, then we get understanding about it.

REM. So that subject holy women would love to reflect this subjection in that economy of blessing in which sovereign love and mercy have set them.

J.T. You see how much pleasure God has in these holy women; such as Sarah and others. God dignifies them in the way they are spoken of; Mary too, and many others that could be cited, all as examples for us now. We have remarkable things mentioned here too, the creation of man and woman in verse 8, "For man is not of woman, but woman of man. For also man was not created for the sake of the woman, but woman for the sake of the man. Therefore ought the woman to have authority on her head, on account of the angels. However, neither is woman without man, nor man without woman, in the Lord". Neither is left alone, each is provided for, but all "in the Lord", and that is the great point that the Lord is stressing, as a warning against the evil of mixed marriages. God undertook to provide a wife for Adam, and if so, why should not He take the same pains as regards ourselves, both sisters and brothers, as to marriage? but they all should be "in the Lord", because the whole economy is in the Lord. Why should anyone break through it for the sake of getting a husband or a wife, breaking through the economy of God, the order of God?

J.Taylor, sr. Ministry, Volume 64 page 71

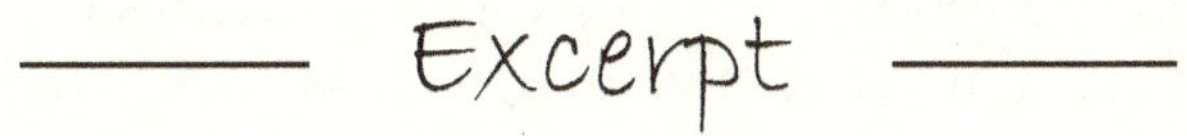

JT: .... These verses in Genesis 24 (61-67), show Rebecca is a person of decision. There is opposition, her brother and mother would detain her, but she is definite. Many are detained from following the Lord by natural influences, but Rebecca is not affected by these; she says, "I will go", and she goes. Her nurse and her maids would accentuate the feminine side, as remarked.

CHH: 'Thou art our sister" (v.60). Does not that thought enter into this as in Canticles, "My sister, my spouse"?

JT: The book of Genesis brings out sisterhood. Sarah is a daughter in the family of Terah, and with Rebecca the thought of sister again comes in. Sisterhood is required for marriage "in the Lord". Spiritually we are by the work of God of the same family as Christ. Rebecca is conscious of the family link with Isaac, as verse 24 indicates.

J.Taylor, sr., Ministry Vol.52 p. 253

The Place and Testimony af Sisters

Psalm 144:11-12, 1 Peter 3:3-6, Judges 4:4-5, 5:24-26, Ruth 3:10-11

In reading these scriptures I had in mind the current exercises of our younger sisters as to the responsible pathway here on earth, in which, as suitable conditions are maintained, God is known as Father and we are His sons and daughters, 2 Cor. 6:17-18.

The younger brothers have been much on our hearts and in our prayers and the Lord has helped them, and He will help the sisters too. Normally accustomed to fill out the divinely ordered place of retirement and comparative obscurity, it seems that a time has come in the ways of God when they may be called upon to leave the shelter of home and move more publicly than has been previously the case. I would encourage our sisters to connect the possibility of the change of circumstances, which they may naturally dread, with the idea of God's displaying the features of His work in His daughters. The exercise of the psalmist was that alien influences were not to mar the beauty of the youth amongst the people of God and that our daughters "should appear as corner-columns, sculptured after the fashion of a palace." The following examples illustrate some of the beautiful features which are to shine in sisters.

Sarah is the first, an old woman, for where else but in the older sisters are the young sisters to find their example? Subjection to her husband is the point stressed, for she called Abraham lord. The allusion is to Genesis 18:12, but all reference to her unbelief is omitted, as in other such references in the New Testament. The point is, I think, how she regarded Abraham in her secret exercises, for it is as she speaks "within herself" that she calls him lord; there is no record that she ever addressed him by this title. She is in her place and marked by instant obedience to her husband's request, ready to have her part in the entertainment of the distinguished visitors, although having servants at her bidding. "Behold, in the tent" is Abraham's answer to the enquiry as to her whereabouts. Her daughters may well follow her example, so helping their husbands to earn divine approval.

Deborah is also a woman of mature age, for she speaks of herself as "a mother in Israel." How valuable are such! The children of Israel came to her for judgment. Her place was unique, and I do not suggest that any sister has such a position today, but I feel the importance of sisters having a judgment of every matter, not passively leaving vital issues to their husbands or the brothers, though never leaving the comely feature of subjection previously mentioned. She is described, in the footnote, as "a woman prophetess," and hence would not be marked by a masculine manner (compare Deut. 22:5). In her well-known song she speaks of Jael, probably a younger woman, her name suggesting agility. She is "blessed above women in the tent." The feature of retirement is still stressed, but with it a dexterity in dealing with evil as it approaches her domain. Her husband appears to be absent and, in his absence, she guards the tent, a position analogous to that of many of our sisters at the present time. We need to pray that the enemy should not get a foothold in such households. What will this sister do? She does not say, "This matter is not for me," but she attacks the evil at its source, most effectively. ' She put her hand to the tent-pin and her right hand to the workman's hammer." This has a spiritual counterpart in the faithful service of Christian women.

Before referring to my last scripture, I would allude to another feature mentioned in the last chapter of Judges. There is "a feast of Jehovah... at Shiloh..." and "if the daughters of Shiloh come out to dance in the dances," I would remind sisters of the need of participation in that, which affords pleasure to divine Persons. Although taking no audible part, save in singing and saying Amen, the wealth of the occasion is dependent on their spiritual emotions being actively engaged. None are to be merely onlookers. These are spoken of as "them that danced."

The foregoing features seem to be connected more with the hidden side of the lives of our sisters. In Ruth, who is spoken of as a "young woman," we have attention called to the known public character of this "daughter," and our desire is that our young sisters, in being brought more publicly into view in the present ordering of God, should have a like character. "All the gate of my people knows that thou art a woman of worth." If the inward features are developed as a result of secret exercise and prayer, we need have no fear but that the outward character will be correspondingly beautiful, and our daughters will indeed appear "as corner-columns, sculptured after the fashion of a palace."

A.J.Ellis, Wood Green, 1942

J.T. ... David said to her, "Blessed be thy discernment", which is a great matter in regard to this point of headship. Then too, when David proposed marriage to her, the feminine thought, involving subjection, is stressed in the persons whom she took. Now the scripture continues, "Every man praying or prophesying, having anything on his head, puts his head to shame. But every woman praying or prophesying with her head uncovered puts her own head to shame; for it is one and the same as a shaved woman. For if a woman be not covered, let her hair also be cut off. But if it be shameful to a woman to have her hair cut off or to be shaved, let her be covered". Then it goes on further, in verse 10, "Therefore ought the woman to have authority on her head, on account of the angels". That is to say, the token of the authority under which she stands, shows that the unseen world, the angels above, are concerned about this matter, and certainly, if they are, all the sisters ought to be concerned about it too. As we read in the Scriptures, the angels have had to say to women as well as to men. Certainly the one that came to Manoah's wife reminds us of subjection in her. He did not come to her husband; he came to her. The husband had to say to him, also, but he hardly shines in what he says to the angel. The angels are thus to be held in regard, for we are told in Hebrews, "Are they not all ministering spirits, sent out for service on account of those who shall inherit salvation?". This matter of salvation includes the idea of headship.

REM. So the thought of subjection is vital and essential to true assembly ground and any service in an assembly setting.

J.Taylor, sr. Ministry Vol. 63 p. 126

The Service of Women

"It is not good that the man should be alone; I will make him a helpmate for him" [lit. a helpmate as his counterpart], was the first announcement of the Lord Jehovah relative to woman's creation, and the place she was designed to fill. Brought by God to Adam, she took her place at his side, as the helpmate of God's providing. The fall came, and she, who was created to be man's partner, was in consequence to be subject to her husband's rule. From Eden they went forth, with the original relation between man and woman unchanged, and the subjection to her husband in consequence of her sins unreversed. She was and is, man's helpmate, however much the original reason of her creation has been lost sight of.

From the fall to the cross we hear nothing of women's right place in creation. The heathen had degraded her into being man's slave. By the law she was protected from being trampled on under certain circumstances (Exodus 21, Leviticus 18:18); yet she never had, under the Mosaic economy, her proper place with man. But after the manifestation of the Second Man [Jesus Christ], and the accomplishment of His work of atonement, the original order of creation is again adverted to, and woman regains her true place with man.

As the glory of man, she has her place by his side, who is the image and glory of God. And, though in Christ Jesus there is neither male nor female, it must ever be remembered that the distinction of sexes, and God's own order of creation respecting them whilst on earth, remains ever the same. "The man is not of the woman, but the woman of the man." Yet she is not to be treated as inferior to man, unfit to be his companion, unsuited for his helpmate; for "as the woman is of the man, so is the man by the woman." Taken out of man at the first, man ever since has been indebted to her for his existence on earth. How these simple statements of the word, if duly pondered, would teach both their true place in relation to each other; and, delivering the woman from that misdirected energy we see around us, lead her to fill that place intended for her by God! In personal service she finds her peculiar sphere, as in public ministry and rule the man has his place; for, the head of the woman being the man, she is not to dishonor her head (i.e., the man) by obliterating the distinction between them; her hair given her for a covering being a standing proof, as we learn from Scripture (1 Corinthians 11), of woman's due subjection to man. Into what minute points can the Spirit enter, commenting even on woman's hair, when God's order is contravened, or the welfare of God's saints imperiled!

In personal service she finds her special sphere; so, when the Lord was on earth, whilst He chose His apostles, and the seventy disciples, and gave them authority respectively to go out and preach, He accepted the un-commanded and un-asked ministrations of women. They ministered to Him of their substance (Luke 8:3). He called His disciples to public service, and made them distribute the bread as they received it from Him, He received the proffered service of women, and was ready, though Lord of all, to be indebted to them for the supply of His own and His disciples' physical needs. As love prompted, they rendered this service, and He as readily accepted it. After His departure we find men as sent by Him were engaged in preaching and teaching, whilst women found an ample sphere in personal service in their families, among the saints, or in helping those who were laboring in the work of God.

Do any ask what were the family duties of Christian women, whether young or old? We have only to turn to Timothy and Titus to find out. If we desire to know how faithful women of old employed themselves, we have several examples handed down to us in the word. The married woman had duties to her husband and children, besides engaging in any labor of love for the saints or the Lord. The unmarried were freer to devote themselves to the things of the Lord. Beyond the range of family ties the sympathies of both could extend themselves. In Jerusalem, Mary, the mother of John, opened her house for prayer on that memorable evening when Peter was miraculously brought out of prison. At Philippi, Lydia of Thyatira hospitably entertained Paul and his company, whilst the elect lady mentioned in 2 John received into her house those brethren that went about ministering the word. Then there was Mary who bestowed much labor on Paul, and the women at Philippi who labored (rather, contended or wrestled) with him in the gospel, There were Tryphena and Tryphosa who labored in the Lord, and the beloved Persis who labored much in the Lord. These holy women, living in that age, and working under the immediate eye of the apostles, found plenty of scope for their energies, and plenty of opportunities for working for their Lord, without forgetting their true place with reference to their head. It was no idle life with them. They were in earnest: they were active. Mary, like her namesakes of the gospel, was forward in personal service: Persis labored much, and those women of Philippi worked zealously with Paul. Exactly what each did is not recorded. Can we not see a reason for this? The service of love may vary in different places and different ages. What is needed at one time may not be needed at another. To wash the feet of the traveler in the East is grateful to the way worn one; in the West such service is not required. Had the special work of each been enumerated, other kinds of service, rendered so willingly and accepted gratefully, might have been thought unsuited for devoted, godly women. The special work of one is recorded – a labor in season as much in our day as in that of Peter – Tabitha made garments and coats. Of others it is only recorded that they labored much. These received the commendation of the apostle, and along with Tabitha have their names preserved in the inspired record. Theirs was service done for the Lord's sake and. accepted by Him.

For those who could engage in a wider field of service than the home circle, or such work as Mary took up, opportunities did not fail them. They might expend time, means, and strength in serving more directly the church. Phoebe, a servant of the church at Cenchrea, "a succourer of many, and of myself also," as Paul writes, is an example of such – probably a person of means, from his description of her, with time, too, at her disposal. She had allotted herself to ministering to the wants of the church at Cenchrea, and the need of individuals who might visit it. Others found a different yet equally wide sphere in which to manifest their womanly devotedness and true love to them. The labors of such are described in 1 Timothy 5:10, Following the example of the Master, they found no service too menial if done to His saints for His sake. How refreshing to see the activity of love displaying itself in these different ways! Love is inventive and fertile in resources, and adapts itself to all that is required.

In these different ways did Christian women find abundant occupation. Real work, healthy activity, untiring devotion, were found perfectly compatible with due subordination to her head, and keeping in the place assigned her by God. As man's helpmate she found work to be done. At home, abroad, or in the church, women found a place which otherwise would have been but indifferently provided for; and she performed duties, suited to her nature, which none but those of her sex could so well discharge. As in Eden, so now in the work of the Lord, and in care of the saints, as well as in domestic life, the helpmate God provided is the fitting help still. Eve was not to take Adam's place, but to be his help, not a substitute but a partner. Women labored with Paul in the gospel, but not in Paul's place.

[no author] From – "Voice to the Faithful," vol. 2, Edited by J.B.Stoney

Excerpt

J.T. It is "a little", showing that it is a question of remnant times; it is not very much, but it is power nevertheless, so we must value it accordingly. The Lord has given it to us and we are doing something; we are all doing a little, the sisters too are doing something in the sense of their minds being at work; they are here sympathetically, which is an immense thing; we should not have such a good meeting without them.

J.Taylor, sr., Ministry Volume 71 page 369

The Prophetesses of Scripture

Exodus 15:20-21, Judges 4:4-9, 2 Chronicles 34:20-24, Luke 2:36-38

You will observe, dear brethren, that these scriptures allude to prophetesses. Other scriptures speak of them also, but these four serve to convey what I understand to be set out in the thought of a prophetess. Others, as I said, are alluded to, some bad ones – for the enemy never fails to imitate what God introduces and uses, so that we have "the woman Jezebel, she who calls herself prophetess", (Revelation 2:20). The most sinister feminine name in the Scriptures is Jezebel. What makes her name so important is that she exists today, and is employing her nefarious powers to the utmost. That she calls *herself* prophetess is significant, for it is a feature of that system to which she belongs, which is essentially Babylonish, and which implies worldly show, worldly distinction, and worldly greatness. Simon called Magus gave out that *he was* "some great one" (Acts 8:9), and Jezebel calls *herself* prophetess. The Spirit of God leaves us in no doubt as to what her prophesying implies, and that its effects are according to what she teaches. Not only are common people her victims, but servants – the Lord's servants: "she teaches and leads astray my servants" – (Revelation 2:20) – teaching them the very worst things. I just allude to her so that we may have in mind what the subject implies; how the enemy uses the idea, and that this personage symbolizes a great religious system, renowned for every iniquity, which has built itself up and spreads its influence abroad.

Then there is another evil prophetess alluded to in Scripture whose name comes down to us; she is called Noadiah. She figured in the days of Nehemiah and harassed him along with others. She is not without her counterpart today; she sought to cause the Lord's servants to be in fear. There are those who harass us with fears of actual dangers so as to weaken our hands. It is a solemn thing to use influence to weaken the hands of those who serve the Lord, so that they should be paralyzed by fear of danger. One is not worthy of the service unless he can face danger, however great; the service implies the will of God. Any influence used to weaken the hands of the servants of God because of danger, is akin to Noadiah, who with Tobiah and Sanballat and others, at that time would interfere with and hamper the servant of God. The work was progressing favorably, and as surely as that is the fact the enemy will do his utmost to hinder. We have to be on our guard that we do not belong to such. Sanballat and others would have Nehemiah to meet them in the plain of Ono, as if he was obliged to do it because of danger. The Spirit of God introduces this prophetess as amongst those who would weaken the hands of Nehemiah.

These are negative features of the subject, and it is sorrowful to own not merely historic, but current dangers. Jezebel and Noadiah, correspond in their characteristics, the latter coming very near to us, and we have to be on our guard that we are not hampering the servants of God by supposing danger. The Lord will stand by those who serve however great the danger, as Paul says, "The Lord shall deliver me from every evil work, and will preserve me", (2 Timothy 4:18).

What I have in mind are the positive features of this subject, and the first prophetess, so called, is Miriam. I am sure it is important to understand this kind of service or ministry, for it is not so much to call attention to the women as serving, but to show that service may, in virtue of power, overcome limitations. Our position, that is, the position of the people of God who love Christ and one another, is a limited position; it is not Pentecost, but a "day of small things" (Zechariah 4:10). It is a day in which the Jezebel spirit in its darkening effect is felt. We are not to call ourselves this or that, we leave that to Jezebel and her kind. Let others call us by what name they will; we cannot control them. God gives us names – names of love. He calls us His children: "See what love the Father has given to us, that we should be called the children of God", (1 John 3:1). We accept joyfully the names and terms of relationship which He gives, but spiritual believers do not give names to themselves.

Yet in spite of the limitation to which I have alluded, a way is made, so that we are not hampered. Thank God! I am not now alluding to the governmental actions of God on our behalf, though He has wrought wonders in this respect, so that we have liberty to meet, as now, without fear. But there is actual power; the Lord says, "I have set before thee an opened door" (Revelation 3:8), but it is because "thou hast a little power". It is a question of *power*, and that has its own significance, it is the power of God. We are released in the sense in which I am speaking, in proportion to our power. Independency imitates the privileges we have, and that surely is no testimony. It is a question of power, and power lifts us out of limitations. Liberty is in proportion to our power.

This word "prophetess" as it appears at the outset, is illustrative of this very thing. Miriam at this time must have been over ninety, from other allusions to her in Scripture. It is the first time she is mentioned by name, and the first time she is called a prophetess. She is said to be sister of Aaron. What I want to show is that while her sex imposed limitations upon her, and more so in the east then than now, she has this dignity, that she is called *the prophetess*, and is also said to be "the sister of Aaron".

She is not regarded officially as Aaron was: Moses was to be God to him, and Aaron was his prophet, whereas there is nothing said about Miriam being appointed. Now what I want to point out in a practical way is, that this ability for service, in one limited by her sex, is indicated by influence for good, and who can deny the scope of influence for good? In whomsoever it is found, influence for good is rare. Miriam's good influence is over the women here. She moves Godward with her timbral. A good lead had been given by Moses in the song, and she is surrounded by the influence of a great victory, and consequently there is liberty. She is more than equal to it; she can join in the song, and that of herself. She does not collaborate with others of her sex to form a party to extend her influence, but she takes her timbral herself and moves. She moves, not as bringing forward something distinctive, but in connection with the great lead that had been given by Moses, and the women went after her. I wish to point out what is meant, for influence for good is to be valued, and way is to be made for it, so that the women went after her with their tumbrels. It was a wonderful movement, but it did not go beyond the women of Israel.

Now you may wonder why I stress this, but I have in mind Miriam's influence as exerted later. You may have influence for good and use it well and effectively, but you may go beyond what is of the Spirit of God. The Spirit of God would teach us how to measure soberly, "according as God hath dealt to every man the measure of faith", (Romans 12:3). We acquire power for good, and, thank God, room is made for it amongst right-minded saints. I may go beyond that, and may sit on it, as a throne, and may become most mischievous unless I maintain self-judgment and discern my proclivities. So, it says in Numbers 12, that Miriam joined with Aaron to traduce the great servant of God, and in that passage, Moses is described as the meekest man on the earth. You see how I may slip into a dangerous line, unless maintained by the Spirit of God. Miriam has influenced a man now – going beyond her province; she is mentioned first in the movement, and she is the only one who became leprous. Aaron is not stricken. She was the prime mover, great person though she was, even though having a place in the leadership according to Micah 6:4. She went beyond her power of influence for good, and became a leader in evil. It was a question of retaining the spirit of smallness and shamefacedness lest we transgress, for as going beyond our measure, we shall certainly come under the discipline of God. I speak of that as a solemn example, not to divert from the good in this sister, but to show how she went beyond her sphere, failing to maintain self-judgment.

Deborah shows another feature in a prophetess. The first as we have seen, is influence for good over those on one's own level. Deborah presents a remarkable picture of this subject; she represents the womanly side. I am not speaking of sisters serving, but of how power lifts out of limitations.

If a sister prays, she is to be covered, recognizing thus the province that belongs to man. If God has given her power, He is not setting aside another principle, so that the covering of the head is the recognition of the ordering of God. That ordering is not violated. But it is sovereign power you find with Deborah. She is a womanly woman. – She is spoken of as "a woman prophetess" (see note in the Darby Translation, Judges 4:4). Christianity is intended to develop what is womanly. Genesis 1:27 tells us "male and female created he them", both terms being given under the idea of "Man".

Christianity has brought about this quality, so in 1 Corinthians 14:20 we read, "in your minds be grown men". This surely applies to every Christian; but to those under authority the instruction is, "Let your women be silent in the assemblies" – but in their silence they adorn the great name of "man". The idea of "man" covers both male and female and that chapter throughout deals with the idea of manhood. Holy women of old adorned the idea; it is a great divine thought which will not come to an end. The idea of male and female will not go into eternity except as regards Christ and the assembly; God will dwell with *men*. It is a divine thought.

Deborah adorns the idea. She dwelt under her own palm tree – it is personal victory – she was living in victory. She was the *wife* of Lapidoth, meaning that she maintained her place, and it says the people came to her for judgment. How can you limit a woman like that? If a woman has judgment and people come to her, how can you limit that? That was between Ramah and Bethel in mount Ephraim. Whether in pressure, or at other times, this rare quality is sure to show itself, and there must be scope for it. As we have noticed in the New Translation, she is called a "woman prophetess", the Spirit of God thus showing the way in which power within limitations is available. How beautiful in the eyes of heaven! In her subjection she is free to serve with a man; she has more wisdom and courage than he, and yet he is going to do the work. All this enters into the position of Barak, and shows how any power that sisters may have is available in the assembly. However weak the brothers are, the power in the sisters is available; Barak would not go without Deborah – and how true she is. She does not offer to go. The power was there, and he had wisdom enough to avail himself of it; the power is in its fulness in spite of the limitations. How great the victory was as a result – proving how much, under such circumstances, can be achieved in the day of small things.

The next prophetess is Huldah. She lived in the days of Josiah. She represents power or ability which is available in limitations, in a crisis, at a time when God is speaking loudly. The book of the law had been lost, but is now recovered, and one is sent to inquire of the Lord. It is a question of the mind of God in a crisis. It is urgent to find out who has it; whatever the limitations we must have it; so, these men, deputed by the king, were sent to inquire of the Lord, and they knew where to go. If there be brothers or sisters who *know*, do not fail to ask such. What is more beautiful about the Lord Jesus – always our Leader – is that at the age of twelve, He is found among the teachers, hearing them and asking them questions. If there be one who can answer, why not ask? Sometimes saints go to the Lord ignoring the provision He makes; but to neglect the saints, is to neglect Him. People say, I have not time to read ministry, but such are despising what He provides. Let us not neglect what God provides.

Huldah was a divine provision at this time. They go to her, the mind of God being there. The prophetic gift goes beyond limitations, because of its value. She was a wife of a certain man, and we get his father and his grandfather named, that is, we are reminded of spiritual lineage in this matter. Let us not despise it; I thank God constantly for the households of the saints, and that the young people are coming under the influence of such teaching. Spiritual ancestry is a great principle with God. Attaching to Huldah, as well as this ancestry, was the keeping of the wardrobe. That is an important matter. One of the most important items in the wardrobe today is righteousness: "Let thy priests be clothed with righteousness" (Psalm 132:9). We have also the clothing of salvation alluded to – priestly vestments these! So many have become exposed by inability to meet obligations – a matter which saints have to face at the present time. We have to accept spiritually, at least, the liability incurred, and if we are keepers of the wardrobe, we shall seek that where needed there shall be self-judgment, so that our brethren may be clothed with righteousness. This is a matter of practical aid, in order that the name of the Lord may be cleared. Huldah is mentioned in connection with this feature of the truth. One would like the brethren to get the idea of the wardrobe. How beautifully it appears in Luke 15! God has great thoughts for us, as a keeper of the wardrobe would know.

Another thing about Huldah is that she was not in the *college*, as the ordinary translation gives it inaccurately, but in the *second quarter* of the town. She did not aspire to a fine house, or to fine things externally, she lived in an inferior part of Jerusalem. She had the mind of God for the moment, and this is of supreme value wherever it may be; and in speaking the word from Jehovah she does not refer to the king in terms of distinction; but says, "tell the man that sent you to me"; she speaks of "the king of Judah" afterwards. How important it is to understand the clothing suited to the time, to avoid show; but to be available in the circumstances as having what is most rare and essential to the testimony of God at the particular moment. The little that any of us may have may be essential to the testimony at the moment.

The final thought is seen in the well-known Anna of Luke 2. Like her sister Miriam, she is an old woman; but the Spirit of God honors her peculiarly; she was a widow of "great age". The allusion is to the honored state of widowhood under these circumstances. She lived with a husband for seven years, and had been a widow for eighty-four years, which tended to add to her lustre. What experience she had! Widowhood, not of itself, but as absorbed in intense interest in the temple, indicates that what was in the temple was everything to her. Need I enlarge upon this, dear brethren? What an element it is in our subject – the element that makes everything of the temple!

Now when we come to very old age, and I think God has in view the old brothers and sisters at the present time, we may thank God for longevity so long as it does not rob the old of ability of perception. Anna had not a dull mind. There was not a woman in Israel like her! If you met her, how buoyant she would be! She departed not from the temple, night or day. Womanliness is not wanting in her; she carried the beautiful traits we have noted, they are all there along with the power that is found in brothers and sisters who are regularly in their position in relation to the temple. They understand things spiritually by frequenting the temple; they do not assume to know because of their age, nor do they occupy you with old things. The temple is not that, it is what is current. I suggest to brethren getting on in years not to acquire the habit of living in the past. Never had the temple at any time had such an honour conferred as at this moment – the Builder of it in the real sense was there, the true Solomon! He was there, yet a Babe, in the arms of the true priest Simeon, who spoke intelligently about Him, and Anna came in. It was her resort, so that she does not miss the greatest occasion.

I press this, lest we should be satisfied with what we already know or be unduly occupied with what we may have had in earlier days. We must be occupied with what God is doing now. The Spirit of God is still here and active. We ought to resolve not to miss any available occasion, that is marked by His presence. We are to be in our places in the assembly; at Pentecost they were *all* together in one place when the Spirit came. Absentees miss the blessing; we may thus miss the greatest thing. Suppose the Spirit of God speaks "expressly" and we miss it! I do not plead for attendance at the meetings only, but also our being alert spiritually. Anna represents the intelligence and power that marks those who habitually recognize the temple. When the great occasion comes, such know how to take part in it. What a warning there is in Barzilai! He had to say, "Can I discern between good and evil? can thy servant taste what I eat or what I drink? can I hear any more the voice of singing men and singing women?"

(2 Samuel 19:35). You may say, 'The young can enjoy that' – but why not you? Let us keep our spiritual hearing, for the Lord addresses Himself to "him that hath an ear". No one can assume to have all the truth. Some special movement of the Spirit of God may come – let us see that we do not miss it – some have done so, and have missed everything for the moment. Let us not be among them. Anna was ready to give praise to God; the intervention of God in Christ was not a surprise to her even at such an age.

This has often been spoken of, but I now treat of it in connection with the subject on hand, – that is, the existence of power, and how it goes beyond limitations, and is available in any given circumstance. May God grant His blessing to each of us!

J.Taylor, sr. Ministry vol. 39

Wives are constantly needed and sought after, which is according to God. Marriages have a great place with Him, a great place in the testimony, that there should be wholly a right seed, Jeremiah 2:21. Hence would-be husbands should approach God as to this, as a matter that concerns Him, and therefore entering into His forethought and consequent provision for such need known to Him beforehand. If this were accepted by brothers and sisters alike, it would preclude mixed marriages, diverse yokes in this sense. It is said, 'whoso findeth a wife findeth a good thing," Prov. 18:22. But then God has forethought as to it, and would thus provide so that the right person may be found. And then parents, as in the following chapters in Genesis, ought to be concerned as to wives for their sons, and husbands for their daughters; the testimony should rule in such exercises and not merely seeking after financial or social advantages.

JT: That is how the matter stands in Genesis. The sisterhood in the family of faith. Paul said that he had a right to lead about a sister as wife; a sister, then a wife. The patriarchs were marked by that, their wives were their sisters before they were their wives.

JT: If a brother is to be used in the service as a gift, it is a matter of great importance to God, and if he is to marry, it should be to someone suitable. He can do everything; why should He not prepare a suitable wife for a brother seeking one?

J.Taylor, sr. Ministry Vol. 48 p. 235

The Service of Man and Woman in the Assembly

1 Corinthians 11:11-12, Romans 16:3-4, Luke 2:25-38

These Scriptures treat of *the man* and *the woman* and that is why I have read them, wishing to show the relative positions and functions of the sexes in the Assembly; and not only to apply these Scriptures in a literal sense, but also to enlarge a little on what is conveyed spiritually in the man and in the woman respectively.

The first Scripture is selected from a chapter which treats somewhat fully of the relative positions of man and woman, and it is not without significance that the chapter also introduces and develops the Assembly in the exercise of its functions in a locality, which, rightly understood, makes room for Christ as the full representation of the man, as the Assembly is the full representation of the woman; and makes room also for the universal position of the Assembly as the one great thought and object of Christ in the current dispensation. The chapter in introducing the Lord's Supper prefaces it by instruction that leads on to the apprehension of the Lord Jesus as Head of the Assembly.

I make a few remarks first as to what belongs to the man, introducing them from the reference to Christ in Revelation 12:5 as the "man child". The better translation gives, "a male son", which seems tautology, but spiritually is full of meaning. A son of course would be a male, but the additional word "male" calls attention to the idea, as absolutely presented in Christ in relation to rule, for it goes on immediately to say, "who shall shepherd all the nations with an iron rod"; that is to say, it is to be rule in an absolute sense. He "shall shepherd all the nations", and shepherding is ruling with skill and with feeling, not arbitrarily, but it is in the "male son" — the word is "*son*" not "child". The idea as seen in Christ is necessarily to be taken on in all relations in which rule, or government is required.

In Judges 4 we have a woman taking the lead in the service

of God in relation to a man: Deborah being the woman, and Barak the man. In the Darby Translation of the Bible, we are told in a footnote, that Deborah is said to be "a woman prophetess". Of course, the word "prophetess" means that she is a woman who prophesied, but in the original the feminine idea is stressed. So that if circumstances amongst the people of God require a sister to take any kind of prominence in the testimony, she never loses her feminineness, she is always a woman; she never takes on the masculine character, for wherever that appears in a sister, you may be sure the flesh is active. If weak conditions require that a sister should become prominent, she never loses her sisterly character; she always has "power" on her head, as 1 Corinthians 11:10 teaches; and that goes forward into the Assembly normally, she never loses her relative position and function, she is always herself.

In speaking thus, I may say that I am impressed that sisters are not functioning as the Lord would have them to, and correspondingly the meetings are wanting in increase. It is no question of alleging that of any particular meeting, but generally it is so. I believe the Lord would call upon the sisters amongst the people of God to take *their* part, and as they do, the idea of the Assembly will come more into evidence. I believe the idea of the Assembly coming into evidence, not theoretically or doctrinally, but practically, is largely dependent on the sisters functioning according to their true relations. If they do, the brothers will not be eclipsed or detracted from in any way, they will the rather be enhanced. Deborah never lost her relative position, she calls upon Barak to act, but the Spirit of God makes it plain that the initiative was with her. She evidently discerned what perhaps we should not have known, were it not that the Holy Spirit tells us hundreds of years later, that Barak had faith. The Spirit of God in Hebrews 11, calls attention to the faith of Barak and says nothing about Deborah. She would, I am sure, accept that as right: she would say, I have more prominence than I should have had; had Barak more energy, I should have less prominence, and that would not have grieved me at all.

From these remarks you will see why I read the two verses in the first Scripture, which say, "For man is not of woman, but woman of man. For also man was not created for the sake of the woman, but woman for the sake of the man". But then, it goes on, "However, neither is woman without man, nor man without woman, in the Lord. For as the woman is of the man, so also is the man by the woman, but all things of God". So that we have set out in the chapter a beautiful order of things; God is regarded as the supreme Head, an appellation first ascribed to Him by David. David says, "Jehovah ... thou art exalted as Head above all", (1 Chronicles 29:11). It awaited the Lord Jesus to come in to set out this wonderful truth, for He not only said things, but He exemplified them. One who contents himself with merely saying things will never be a model: if I *show* a thing, it is established in the mind. The Lord Jesus set out this great principle of God — headship, as I might call it, in His life here — "The head of Christ is God", and "Christ is the head of every man, but woman's head is the man... but all things of God".

There is a beautiful position set out for us in the passage, which is to be seen in every phase of life, in the household, and everywhere; wherever men and women are together according to God, this great truth will be seen, and God is pleased and glorified in it. If there is one thing one cherishes more than another, it is to afford God a little pleasure. In the life of Jesus it was constant, and now in the Assembly this great thought of graded headship set out in any way is highly pleasing to God. It is the order that He has ordained and it is pleasing to Him as He sees it; and the angels see it too, it is a spectacle for heaven, leading to that remarkable statement in Ephesians 3:10, that "the all-various wisdom of God" is to be seen now in the Assembly by "the principalities and authorities in the heavenlies". What moral victory there is for God in His people as His thoughts are in any little way expressed in them!

I wish now to show how it is worked out in a man and his wife, for Scripture affords us concrete examples of its teaching. As I said, things are not only told to us, but *shown* to us. Here we have it in a man and his wife, Aquila and Priscilla: this couple has a unique place in Scripture in several respects, but in particular, that they are never mentioned apart, they are always seen together. I need not say that there is *some* suggestion of Christ and the Assembly in that: were we to understand the position we should see that Christ, normally being its Head, is always seen in relation to the Assembly. Of course He has His place and glory as in the Deity in which the creature can have no part, but as Man in heaven having effected redemption, the Assembly is His body, His wife indeed, and in this sense He and she are inseparable. This marks the present time and gives a special character to the dispensation. In the future too it will appear. Aquila and Priscilla are mentioned six times, always together. The suggestion fits in with Paul's ministry, this man and his wife being specially identified with the apostle.

First of all, they are introduced to us as in Corinth, they were of a certain craft; apparently both occupied in the same craft — tent-makers. It seems that they worked together, and Paul joined them — not because they were Christians, it does not say that; but "because they were of the same craft" (Acts 18:3). All this comes in where the great thought of the Assembly is worked out locally, that is Corinth.

Aquila and Priscilla are mentioned three times together in Acts 18. The idea of wisdom would be there; the first epistle to the Corinthians shows that the idea of divine wisdom was prominent in Paul's service there, and Priscilla would not fail to suggest that "The wisdom of women buildeth their house", (Proverbs 14:1). Wisdom is a feminine word; the feminine idea in this sense leads to the Assembly. "The wisdom of women buildeth their house; but folly plucketh it down with her hands". So that you can understand how that thought would be present, at least to the mind of Paul, as to Priscilla — what a fine sister she was! I am speaking of her because of the way she is mentioned in these different references. Her name appears first as *often* as Aquila's does. You will find, "Aquila and Priscilla", and then "Priscilla and Aquila", and then you find "Aquila and Priscilla", and then again "Priscilla and Aquila"; is that accidental? No, it is educational: that is to call attention to what is *possible*, and what is possible should always be aimed at; it should never be regarded as impossible. If it were possible in these two, it is possible in any two, and it is possible in Christ and in the Assembly as His body. So that we find these two, as I said, interchangeably having precedence one of the other. Not that Priscilla would ever *take* precedence of her husband: were we to enter their house — and we are told that there was an Assembly in their house — that Assembly would be adorned, as I may say, by the seemliness and the grace of this sister, Priscilla. She would never becloud, she would never stand in the light of her husband: he would the rather shine in her graces, for the woman is *of* the man.

That great principle is set out in Genesis 2 how often it is spoken of at our marriage meetings, and rightly! I do not say Adam suffered, but certainly he had an extraordinary experience, and that is a deep sleep, not an ordinary sleep, but a *deep* one; the allusion, of course, is to the death of our Lord Jesus Christ. And Jehovah takes a rib, and out of that rib He builds a woman. That word "build" is a remarkable word, it is the first time it is used in Scripture. It is not applied to the universe; the word "framed" (Hebrews 11:3) is used there. Building implies special skill, and belongs to the woman. This was one of the items of the work of the sixth day, the greatest work-day of all — and God presents her to the man. What will the man say about it? He was asleep when it was done apparently, but he *knew*; he could name all the other creatures, and he named this one. And there it is: as one remarked elsewhere, He lost a rib, but it is given back to him a thousand-fold: he lost nothing, he gained. But then, this gain should not be merely theoretical, it should be practical in the Assembly — in the household, of course, in every sphere of life, but specially in the Assembly. In the highest thought of it, it is a question of what the Assembly is to Christ, but then it should be seen surely in the practical working out of the Assembly, in the sisters in relation to the brothers.

Now I want to show briefly how all this is foreseen in the gospels, for the gospels are generally to support what we have in the Acts and the epistles. So, Luke gives us two persons at the beginning; as the Lord Jesus is brought to Jerusalem to the temple, these two are there. The early chapters in this gospel should be studied in relation to our subject. Luke only, mentions these two persons, and I believe no brother is in the Assembly save as he understands what is presented in Simeon, and that no sister is in the Assembly save as she understands and moves according to what is seen in Anna — they are models.

First of all, as regards Simeon, you have the word "behold" — "behold, there was a man in Jerusalem whose name was Simeon". He is not an ordinary man, but one distinguished as spiritual. He looked for Christ, he was a man of *hope*, a man who counted on what God had said; he expected God to do what He had said. But then he was a man *in Jerusalem*: now that is not an ordinary circumstance; the preposition "in" there means more than simply circumstance; it is characteristic, and it enters into the position of the brothers in the Assembly. He is not only local. Of course, Jerusalem is a locality, but it had a place that no other earthly city ever had or ever will have; it had a metropolitan position, it was the divine center. "A man in Jerusalem" was in the very center of what God was doing — that is the point. The facts mentioned show it applied characteristically. I speak thus, dear brethren, so that we might become less local and more general. That is, that we may be in the very center of things, our position is there, we are concerned about everything that concerns God, whether it be general or local, whether it be fifteen thousand miles away or local — we are in the center of things. There is very little of this attitude amongst us. Were there more of it, we would support what is general in every way we are able.

I need not now enter into the many ways in which we may support what God is doing, say in China or in New Zealand or Australia; for China is not in principle any more to God than New Zealand is — let us not forget that; God is no respecter of persons. He never intends the promotion of what is popularly called "missionary". What is missionary *properly* means persons sent out by the Holy Spirit on whom the hands of the Assembly are placed, they are released, let go by the saints, and they are "sent forth by the Holy Spirit", and then they go. It does not say where they were sent; what follows in Acts 13 is the record of where they *went*; they went down to Cyprus, through the island, etc., etc. I say that by the way, that we may not take on the characteristics of what is around us, that we may be able to stand against what is current religiously. We are so prone to take it on. There are those who would give a hundred pounds with a view to Chinamen being converted, who would not give a cent for the conversion of Englishmen! I say that advisedly. I would desire to be in full sympathy with all that God is doing: a man in Jerusalem is concerned about what God is doing *wherever* it is.

To return to Simeon a certain thing was revealed to him "by the Spirit"; that is to say, he recognized the Spirit; he is dependent on the Spirit for his understanding of things. "It was divinely communicated to him by the Holy Spirit, that he should not see death before he should see the Lord's Christ": until he had seen the Man who should do everything for God: he was expecting Him, and he went by the Spirit into the temple, and the Child is brought in and he takes Him in his arms. The facts are known to us; I am only referring to them now to draw attention to this brother brought forward by Luke, as I verily believe, to show us that our setting is not simply in our houses or our businesses, but, so to speak, in *Jerusalem*; it is a spiritual position. I am in it spiritually, and I come into the temple spiritually, and in the temple I receive Christ. His being brought is characteristic; there is always someone to bring Him in. The thought is, of course, that *I* should bring Him in. Here He was brought in by His parents, which, of course, is literal and historical. It may be that a brother just converted has some little thought of Christ, and a spiritual man takes this little thought — I say "little" because the Lord Jesus here is just a Babe — and magnifies it, he makes it of use universally. What a service that is! And how beautifully he speaks; he says, "Lord, now thou lettest thy bondman go, according to thy word" — He is regulated by the word; it is no mere sentimental thought, as often expressed by people who say they want to die, and the like: it is a question of the word of God, the mind of God for each of us — "for mine eyes have seen thy salvation, which thou hast prepared before the face of all peoples; a light for revelation of the gentiles and the glory of thy people Israel". That is the brother! He is able to take up any thought of Christ that comes into the Assembly by whomsoever, and give it its proper setting, give it, perhaps, a universal bearing; here it is a question of the light of God concerning the gentiles, and the glory of His people Israel. How the whole scene was lit up with Simeon's remarks! There never was such a time before in the temple.

Then, without going into detail: Anna came in at the same hour, that is to say, the sister is not absent, she is there, and this has the significance of being an example for us. How beautifully Anna comes in and shines! She does not take the Child in her arms; that had already been done. Hers is another part in the service. He is in the proper position in the arms of Simeon. She comes in at the same hour: she praises God. The Spirit of God does not give us Simeon's age, but He gives us a clue as to Anna's age, and I do not think any of us will lose anything if we try to work out how old she was. Every moment of this woman's life is spiritually interesting.

I would like to be such as that, that the brethren, if they have to talk of me at all, can talk of me from the beginnings of my history. What can they say about the beginnings? And then the middle life? and the late life? When God writes up His people, He goes back to their birth (Psalm 87). Anna "lived with her husband seven years from her virginity" and she was "a widow up to eighty-four years". If the Spirit of God wished us to know definitely how old she was to the minute, as we say, He could have told us how old she was, but He wishes us to have an insight of her whole life. She might have been

106 years old — one might figure it out that way: but every moment of that woman's life was spiritually interesting. And now at the end she does not miss the greatest privilege that the temple of God had afforded, nor can any one of us afford to miss it.

One great secret of the spiritual poverty amongst us is that we do miss such occasions, and we do not feel we miss them. We cannot afford to miss what goes on in the Assembly. The Assembly is a place of wonders; the Spirit of God is in it. If we have spiritual eyes to see and ears to hear we shall see and hear wondrous things, as Manoah and his wife saw the angel do wondrously (Judges 13). Anna did not miss the presence of Christ in the temple, she came in then and she "gave praise to the Lord"; and the Spirit of God tells us she did not depart from the temple; serving night and day with fastings and prayers. And now, when the great moment arrives, she is present and makes the most of it, adds to it, and "spoke of him to all those who waited for redemption in Jerusalem". Jerusalem, as I said, represents the center of the whole realm of God's interests. How wide her outlook was! We are told whose daughter she was; she was the daughter of Phanuel, and to what tribe of Israel she belonged, that is Asher. These are points of great interest. Asher was to be possessed of sons: although she was a daughter, she was spiritually a son; she was marked by the dignity and liberty spiritually that belongs to sonship. His bolts were to be iron and brass — there was strength and compactness about her, and her feet were dipped in oil (Deuteronomy 33:24-25).

We have often heard these things, but they are very apropos to what is before us now — that the sisters should be marked by the features seen in Anna. She came in contact in some way with all those who looked for redemption in Jerusalem. She spoke of *Him* — she was no gossiper, no idler; she was a son of Asher engaged in the temple service and in speaking of Christ to all who looked for redemption in Jerusalem. May God bless the word.

J.Taylor, sr., Ministry, vol.39 p. 238

Maids

2 Kings 5:2-3, 2 Samuel 17:15-17, Acts 12:12-15, Psalm 46:1-11

The first three scriptures that we have read make reference to maids. I wondered if we could think about that. If anyone thinks "This cannot apply to me" I would say that what we have before us would have application to everyone. We may be speaking about maids and it may be that there is something that has particular reference to the young sisters, but it would apply to each one of us. We see that in that the apostle Paul's desire for a locality, Corinth, was to present them a chaste virgin to Christ. That was to be the characteristic of the whole locality and it was to be the characteristic therefore of everyone in it so that they could be presented with virgin affections to Christ, Christ being the one object for them. So, it would apply to each one of us.

The first scripture especially would have reference to everyone. We see this little maid. We spoke earlier about what was little and now we have a little maid. I would like to commend her to you as an example for you. The first thing is that she had knowledge of a man in another place who was the answer to the problem in the place where she was. Now perhaps you know the Lord Jesus as your Saviour, but I would like to be assured that everyone here knows that they have a link with Christ as a Man in another world who has the answer to all the problems that are in this world. This girl could point to the prophet; he was not there; he was, in type, in another world. Do you know Christ as a person in another world, who is interested, and who has the solution? It may be a problem in your own life, whatever it may be at the moment, or it may be a problem in someone else's life, but you can point to Him. He, in His place of exaltation, is the One who has the answer. The answer here was to the problem of leprosy, sin and all its evidences. And we look forward to the time when this scene will be changed because Christ has exercised His right to take control and to put things right. Everything will be in order. That does not prevent you, or anyone you come into contact with, being put in order now, through a link with a Man in another world.

Another important thing about the little maid is that not only did she have a link with a man in another world but she knew that she belonged to that world. Do you realise that you are a heavenly person? Have you ever thought of that? You may say, "These things that affect us in this world seem to affect me: if it is too hot, I am too hot, if it is too cold, I am too cold". But do you know yourself as a heavenly person? Do you know that that is where you belong? You may say, "I am always doing things that I do not really want to do, that are sin; I do not feel very heavenly". But do you know that you are a heavenly person? If you belong to Christ, if you have a link with that Man, you are a heavenly person. That is what should be in your heart. Have you the assurance that you belong there? You do not belong to this scene, you do not belong to this world, to this earth, you belong to heaven. From that basis you will find the power to behave more like a heavenly person. If you try to struggle to be heavenly you will struggle all your life and get nowhere. You must begin knowing that you are heavenly. Do you know that you are a heavenly person? Do you know in your soul that you are heavenly, that heaven is where your home is? We sing that: 'Yon heaven is our home' (hymn no 7). But do you only sing it or do you know it? Does it characterise you, that you know that you are a heavenly person?

A third feature of this little maid is that she has depths of feelings. Reference was made in the reading to the little children crying (see Matthew 21:15). She gives a cry, a more intelligent cry than would come from little children: "Oh, would that my lord were before the prophet that is in Samaria!". She knew the answer for herself and she knew that she could point it out to another. It is very clear that if a little maid could do this for a great man in the world like Naaman, you can do it. Whoever you are, brother or sister, young or old, you can do what this little maid did. You can present the glad tidings. You can tell people that there is a Man in heaven who has the power to be the solution to air the problems in this scene and to the problems in their lives. This little maid is an evangelist, she does the work of an evangelist, and you are not excluded from the word, "do the work of an evangelist", 2 Tim 4: 5.

In the second scripture we have some very imposing persons. We have Hushai, the king's friend, who was very close to the king, who could give good advice, and who enjoyed the favour and the presence of the king. There were Zadok and Abiathar the priests, and there were these two young men Jonathan and Ahimaaz who were the sons of the priests – all very important persons. There was a problem, a message had to be sent. And there was one other very important link in the chain – without it they could not have done anything - and that was a maid. Are you available to do just what is needed? It would be a dangerous thing to do: the city was in Absalom's control; the usurping king was in charge there. If she had been captured what would have happened? She would have been imprisoned, she might have been killed; but she was willing and she was reliable. Are you a reliable person? Young sister, young maid here, are you reliable? Could the brethren depend on you? We know that there is only one person that we can depend on absolutely and that is Christ. But are you sufficiently formed after Christ that the Lord and the brethren could depend on your being reliable? She must have some of the characteristics of the little child in the fact that her name is never mentioned. Among all these imposing people there is no suggestion that she wanted to be famous. She did not want to be known she was just available for service. One of the footnotes in the New Testament is about a sister who did the needed service (see Romans 16:1). Can you think of anything better? She did the needed service. Of one other woman it is said by the Lord: "What she could she has done", Mark 14:8. She was one that was reliable. Ask yourself whether you would be able to put your name in here. There is no name here; could you put your name in as the reliable person on whom all would depend so that the message would get through?

Rhoda we have another maid, in very difficult circumstances. Peter who had the leading place in the testimony at the time was imprisoned, so the brethren gathered together to pray. This young sister is with the brethren coming together to pray, which is a very commendable thing: when the brethren pray this young sister was there with them. That is good. It may be that we sometimes think that it is more important for the brothers to be there when it is time for prayer, but although they express prayer it does not reduce the importance of the sisters being there on our occasions for prayer. It is very important that they should be there. That would be one important feature of this maid, she was there when the saints were gathered. Peter knocks at the door, and Rhoda goes to answer it. It is very interesting that she should do that, because it was the middle of the night. The brethren were all gathered together. From experience, if somebody was knocking at the door of the meeting room when we were in prayer, it would be one of the brothers who would go out, especially if it was dark. Yet at night, despite all the dangers, she was willing to do whatever was needed. She was willing to get up and listen. She was a good listener. That is another good thing – to be a good listener. You may not be able to do things but you can listen. Are you a good listener? She recognised the voice of Peter. If I could make application of that too, it is important to be able to recognise the Lord's word that is coming at any given time. It is not only important that the older brothers and those who take responsibility in speaking should know what the Lord's word is but you should as a younger person, a young sister. You should be able to recognise the Lord's word for the moment. At this time, it was coming through Peter, and she listened; she was a good listener.

We come to the very serious matter that the brethren, when she reported that Peter was standing before the entry, said to her "Thou art mad". They had been praying for his release and when they received the answer it did not come in the way they thought it would and they did not accept it. Are you prepared to be ridiculed in your locality when you are right? You might say, "There are all these older brothers and we can depend on them, they are sure to know what is right; there are older sisters who have spent a long time in prayer, we would expect them to be right". But it is not for you to put the responsibility on someone else. It is not for you to say, 'These older brethren should know what is right'. You should know yourself, however young you may be, whether you are a brother or a sister. I would put it straight-forwardly to the younger sisters that you should bear in mind this possibility that you could be the only person who is right. The brethren might say that you were mad - a very severe matter. But did she say, "These brethren must be right; I cannot be right"? No; she maintained that it was so. She maintained it because she knew by experience, she knew Peter, she knew his voice and she could maintain it. She maintained that it was so. Would you be willing, would you have the strength to be the one to maintain the truth? We all trust that it will never come to that and you will never be put to this test but it is a possibility. It happened here in these early days when things were in a sense publicly bright. Young sister, are you ready to fill in that breach, to know the truth and to maintain the truth? Do not leave it to others. Do not say we can depend on such and such a brother to lead us through, he is well taught, he knows the truth. Can you maintain it yourself?

The Psalm that we read is interesting too. You may wonder what the connection is. The connection is in the heading; it says it is "On Alamoth" and if you look through the footnotes you will find that it is the voices of young women. This Psalm was composed by persons with great experience with God but the response was in voices of young women. That should characterise every one of us; that our response to God should be as a chaste virgin to Christ. It should be in the freshness and depth of affection that one would expect to characterise young women. We cannot exclude anyone from this. It has its particular reference to you, whoever you are, whatever your age. It also would be right to apply it individually, particularly to a young sister. You come to the meetings and we appreciate that there is a little bit of a problem since you do not have any active part in speaking, and you do not have active part in giving out hymns, but that does not exclude you from the praise. It does not mean that it is only the brothers who praise because they are the ones who express it. When a brother is speaking on his feet it does not exclude you from the praise. God is expecting praise from you. He is expecting praise from your heart. Praise is not what is said exactly, it is what is from your heart. Your heart should be active in response. You can have part in singing, you are not just following someone else's lead. We sometimes, every one of us I expect, find that we are singing the words and our hearts are not in what we are singing. We need help about that, we can all easily sing the words and our spirits not be involved. It is for each one of us to have our spirits involved, to have our hearts involved in what we are singing. There should be something of this virgin affection of response for Christ.

I do not intend to go into much detail about this Psalm. It speaks of God as a refuge "a help in distresses, very readily found". What do you do if you are in distress? You cry. That was the word that came in earlier. Do you cry to the Lord when there is need? It goes on to an appreciation of the river "the streams whereof make glad the city of God". Do you have an appreciation of the Holy Spirit for His help to you in your part in the testimony? "Make glad the city of God"; He makes glad. Does He make your heart glad? Are you gladdened by the Spirit when He speaks to you of Christ? Think of Rebecca as she went across the wilderness, how glad she would be to have her affections awakened to the man Isaac. The servant would bring out the glories and perfection of Isaac, in type the heavenly man, the man that she would be connected with. She already was connected with him, kindred to him. It goes on to an appreciation in this Psalm of what will not be seen literally until the world to come. Are you interested in the world to come? This Psalm speaks in the past tense of some of these things; "behold the works of Jehovah, what desolations he hath made in the earth: He hath made wars to cease". We look around and we see that there are plenty of wars, though we are thankful for what there is of peace that has been maintained in this continent for so long. That is in the ways of God and we are thankful for it. But we look forward to Christ's day. Are you interested in the world to come, in what we refer to as the millennium? That would be something for you to consider. What will the answer be, what will be their response to God? "Jehovah of hosts is with us; the God of Jacob is our high fortress. Selah". Consider these things, give a response.

I trust we will all think about this, give consideration, which is what 'Selah' would suggest. We have spoken of several things this morning, spoken of Christ, spoken of the way that you can be faithful to Him, whether young or old, whether brother or sister. Remember that this is what the Lord has in mind - that you should have your part in the testimony and have your part in response to Him. What is the end when we speak of little children? It is response. What is the end if we speak about the maid? It is response - response in affection for Christ. Let us all be marked by response to Christ, every one of us, for His Name's sake. Amen.

David C.Brown, London, England 1990.
From – "A Word in its Season" #212.

Collection of Excerpts

How God Prepares a Dwelling for Himself Among His People

Exodus 1:21; Exodus 2:1 - 3; Exodus 15:20, 21; Exodus 35:25, 26

We see here that the enemy's purpose was to destroy the spiritual family. This family was called Hebrews, which indicated that they were suffering reproach. As those being born of God and having the Spirit of God, even we suffer reproach, and the enemy would destroy all such. At the present time it is not through literal death he seeks to destroy us, but through the influence of the world. God is carrying out a work in the hearts of His people, and this in view of preparing a shelter for the young and the newly converted ones. It is when the spiritual life in a soul begins to appear that the enemy endeavours to destroy it. Therefore the young converts need the greatest care. They do not know to what dangers they are exposed, but we, who are older, know. These two women received special blessing from God. One does not need special gift to care for the young, but more a spiritual instinct, wishing to protect the new life that is in them. God will specially honour and encourage such a service, for it says that God dealt well with them and built them houses. What a precious thought this is, that God will give spiritual increase on account of this service, as we, in spite of the enemy's bidding, have sought to protect the spiritual life in the young, that there might be found an Israel of God according to the word of the apostle: "And as many as shall walk by this rule, peace upon them and mercy, and upon the Israel of God". In the eyes of the enemy we are regarded with reproach like Hebrews, but in the eyes of God we are the Israel of God.

In the second chapter we read of the mother of Moses that she saw him that he was fair. The midwives did not take into consideration whether the children were fair or not. They saved the male children, but for the mother of Moses it was the fairness of the child which was of such importance, as it says in Hebrews 11, that they saw the child beautiful. This was, of course, another reason why they should protect the child. All believers are fair and pleasing in the eyes of God, even if this trait has not yet come out in them, for God knows the end from the beginning. As those who are born of Him, we shall all be fair, for we shall all be like Christ. When Gideon asked the kings of Midian about his brethren they answered, "As thou art, so were they; each one resembled the sons of a king". In the light of all this we see of what value the saints are, and how important it is that we should protect them against the enemy. This woman hid the child; she protected it from the enemy's influence and power. We find in this woman the principle of preserving what is of God from the power of the enemy. Young believers are in a special way exposed to the enemy's power through the influence of the world. In type the mother of Moses delivered the child to death. This corresponds to what we do when we let a child come under the water of baptism, the type of the death of Christ. When Moses was put into this ark of bulrushes which was prepared with such care, he was saved. We may say that even the daughter of Pharaoh had something of this woman's spirit about her. She was in her mind quite unlike the others in her father's house; she showed mercy.

When one goes about amongst the people of God one perceives what great lack there is of gift to preach the gospel and even of ability to serve the people of God. But if this secret womanly service that ought to characterise every one of us, brothers as well as sisters, is found amongst us, we should find that young people would grow up in our midst, and they would be furnished with gifts. Another thing that we find in Exodus is that they who served God did not fear the wrath of the king. It says of the parents of Moses that they did not fear the injunction of the king. They did not obey it in spite of the consequences. And it says of Moses that he did not fear the wrath of the king. This service requires courage.

The next woman we may consider is Miriam. She is mentioned by name for the first time here in Exodus 15, and she is called a prophetess. She was no doubt, Moses' sister, the one who watched over him when he lay in the ark in the sedge of the Nile. Very early she commenced this service of which I have been speaking, but now we find that she is called a prophetess. It is obvious that she was an old woman here, older than both Aaron and Moses. We find even that she had grown in her soul. It is something remarkable that a woman should be a prophetess. God would not use any person to represent Him and make known His thoughts if he was not characterised by His features. Miriam had, no doubt, for a long time walked with God in secret, and therefore she could be called a prophetess, and not only this, but we read that she took the tambour in her hand and led the women in song. We see that she had a great influence over the other women, for they all went out after her with tambours and with dances. When we consider how many women there were in Israel then, we understand what influence she had.

It is of great importance to exercise a good influence over the people of God. They all followed her, and she did not lead them astray. It is, alas, possible for a sister or a brother to lead the people of God astray. It is most sorrowful when one having influence amongst the people of God leads them astray. But he who by his influence is able to lead the people of God in the right path is of the greatest value amongst the saints. We see here how all the women went after her. They followed her with music which speaks of something that calls forth response from our hearts. It is important to have understanding in the things of God, but it is great value to be able to call forth spiritual feelings in the people of God; and this was what Miriam did here. When we come together as we do at this time or in one another's houses, our hearts are moved with spiritual things and spiritual feelings. This is a feature that enters into the peace-offering. There is a state of spiritual joy coming in amongst the saints, and the meetings are not dull but vigorous and characterised by refreshment and holy joy. The Lord gets His portion in all this. We see here that all the women are in this, and it says that Miriam answered them: "Sing to Jehovah, for he is highly exalted: the horse and his rider hath he thrown into the sea". So that in Miriam we find the ability of calling forth the best feelings, and she is also able to give an answer; she apprehends the position: "Jehovah ... is highly exalted". Here we see the full result of the work which the midwives commenced, but now it is no longer a service in secret, it is a public service, for the enemy was conquered, and God was exalted.

The final thought I had in mind is found in chapter 35 where the great result comes out, that is, the tabernacle and the women's part in the making thereof. It says, "And every, woman that was wise-hearted spun with her hands". We come now to a work done with hands, a work that had the dwelling of God in view. All this, dear brethren, is something which ought to be found in every local place where the saints are, for if we save the saints from the enemy, and if we protect the spiritual family and call forth the innermost feelings of their hearts, then all this is in view of God having a dwelling here. Every woman who was wise-hearted spun with her hands, and she brought what she had spun. It was the work of hands, it was a personal service with their hands, and therefore they brought it, the blue and the purple, scarlet and byssus. Later it says: "Every man and woman whose heart prompted them to bring". Here we see that it came from their hearts. The Holy Spirit sheds abroad the love of God in our hearts with the result that we love God, and our hearts move us so that we desire there should be a dwelling for God here.

From all this we see, dear brethren, how these women speak to us of the great result that is in view in Exodus. We find the family of God, saved from the world, preserved in spiritual life. Thus we see how the innermost feelings and love of the saints come out, and at last the work which we can do with our hands, so that God might have a dwelling amongst us as it says in Ephesians: "In whom ye also are built together for a habitation of God in the Spirit".

J. Taylor, sr., Ministry Vol. 75 p. 108

Now Deborah, who speaks of herself very soberly and humbly in chapter 4, refuses to take the lead, but puts Barak forward -- a fine example for sisters. She did all she could to make a poor leader a good one, and she succeeded. It is within the province of the sisters to do this, to so compass the brothers, to so move, as to convey to them the place which is theirs as head and to take up that place. "I will by all means go with thee" (Judges 4:9), she said, but he was to take the lead. She put him forward and he went forward. "Up", she says, and Barak went forward, and there went up at his feet ten thousand men. And Deborah went with him. She had said to Barak, "I will by all means go with thee, only that it will not be to thine honour upon the way which thou goest" (Judges 4:9). Hundreds of years afterwards he gets credit, for it says in Hebrews 11 that Barak had faith. But Deborah said, "Jehovah will sell Sisera into the hand of a woman" (Judges 4:9). Barak later pursues Sisera, and is shown into the tent of Jael. She says, "Come, and I will shew thee the man whom thou seekest, ... and behold, Sisera lay dead, and the pin was in his temples" (Judges 4:22). Spiritually it is one of the finest of exploits, but it was Jael's, not Barak's. Sisera, the enemy's great leader, is nailed through his head to the ground, for it is a question of evil headship, and hence the way is now cleared for the opening up of headship and leadership according to God. We can thus understand how fitting it was that this remarkable saint, Deborah, should lead in song.

Can we not picture this triumphant scene? There is Barak, Deborah, possibly Jael, and others, devoted servants of God, joining in this collective singing. Deborah and Barak sang; not that they merely composed a song, but they sang it. It was a singing matter. No doubt they composed it, the hymn or the song, or Deborah did; but the point is that they sang it, and the first thing they mention in the song is that leaders led . The Authorised Version is at fault in verse 2 of Judges 5. The thought is that leaders led, that is to say, there is a class called leaders, and the book of Judges emphasises that if one is a leader in name, he is to be one in reality. "For that leaders led in Israel", sings Deborah, "Bless Jehovah!" It is a beautiful tribute to God. The theme of the song is to show that divine power enables the people of God to come through conflict to victory, and what fills the mind of the singers at the outset is that leaders led . It was a triumphant thought to Deborah; not that she considered herself to be the leader, and yet she was. But there was Barak; through her skill, grace, influence, and prophetic power, she had put him forward; showing that the saints can under God accomplish such things. It is within our province to encourage those who are leaders, that they might truly lead.

J.Taylor, sr., Minisytry Vol. 43 p. 435

QUES: Why was the prophetic word given to Rebecca and not carried on to Isaac?

JT: She had right family exercises, as we have seen, and these were honoured by God. Isaac should have profited by the prophetic word to his wife. We may be sure she did not hide it from him. How much comes before us in the prophetic meetings, ministry that we like, but we do not seem to profit by it! You cannot imagine that Rebecca did not tell Isaac of this prophetic word which she had from Jehovah. Isaac should have said at once, "I must not, then, let my mind rest on Esau'.

QUES: In chapter 28 (Genesis), "Isaac called Jacob", verse 1. Do you not think that Isaac is quite recovered here in regard to the right man?

JT: Yes, but it seems it was through his wife. He would have let things drift.

REM: With regard to mixed households, what great care was taken in relation to Rebecca's genealogy! If a man marries an unspiritually-minded young woman what can he expect in after life in the government of God? Reference is made to who Rebecca was; very particular care was taken along that line.

JT: Yes. If Isaac had an unspiritual wife, where would he have gone in this matter? She saved him, and no doubt that is why her genealogy is mentioned. She belongs to the feminine side, which represents the sisterhood that God provides for His people; so that it is said that she is "the daughter of Bethuel the Syrian of Padan-Aram, the sister of Laban the Syrian," chap.25:20. There is no question as to who she is, the whole of chapter 24 stresses it. She was carefully selected on spiritual lines. Where would Isaac have been in this crisis with an unspiritual wife? Rebecca does not support him in loving a man of the field, she stands by the man of God's purpose.

REM: Scripture speaks of husband and wife being 'fellow-heirs of the grace of life", 1 Peter 3:7. One of the great wedges that Satan tries to get in is difference of thought in regard to the children, so that prayers are hindered.

JT: Yes. You are referring to Peter: 'that your prayers be not hindered." If Isaac and Rebecca prayed in the morning there would be a dark spot, because Isaac would be praying for Esau, ignoring his unbelief and worldliness. What darkness there would be in that!

REM: Rebecca's father is the eighth son of Nahor, she is the product of the eighth son.

JT: She is thoroughly qualified as to the sisterhood. She comes in immediately after we have Isaac raised from the dead, chap.22:20-23. She is thoroughly of the sisterhood that God has provided for His people, that is spiritual women.

QUES: What are we to learn from the activities of Rebecca in promoting the furthering of the prophetic word, and the subterfuge she used?

JT: The point is that she is an exercised woman, a spiritual woman. She has had a revelation from God and is maintaining the effect of it. She is equal to it. The subterfuge is to be deplored, but she does take the ground of laying down her life for the truth, "On me be thy curse, my son," chap.27:13. She is ready to take on the curse, ready to die, we may say for the truth of God, so that the prophetic word might go through. It must go through, and that is what Paul means in Romans 9:11, "that the purpose of God according to election might abide." She would die for that- 'the purpose of God according to election." Every exercised sister or brother would stand by that at all costs.

REM: So Rebecca steps in when Isaac is going to continue in his failure in chapter 27, and saves the situation again. It says, "And it came to pass when Isaac had become old, and his eyes were dim so that he could not see, that he called Esau," verse 1. The situation is saved by Rebecca stepping in for God, telling Jacob what to do.

JT: Yes. Chapter 27 shows how Rebecca's spirituality continues. She is not one who is spasmodically spiritual, but, in principle, continually so, and she saves the position and saves Isaac by her devotion to the truth. She hears what he says to Esau. Think of the speech Isaac makes to Esau! "And it came to pass when Isaac had become old, and his eyes were dim so that he could not see, that he called Esau his elder son, and said to him, My son! And he said to him, Here am I. And he said, Behold now, I am become old; I know not the day of my death. And now, I pray thee, take thy weapons, thy quiver and thy bow, and go out to the field and hunt me venison, and prepare me a savoury dish such as I love, and bring it to me that I may eat, in order that my soul may bless thee before I die," Gen.27:1-4. Think of a man who is an object of the counsels of God speaking about the weapons of a sportsman, saying of meat, "such as I love"! It is very humbling. But verse 5 goes on to say, "And Rebecca heard when Isaac spoke to Esau his son. And Esau went to the field to hunt venison, to bring it." She was the saving element. Evidently she is on the alert and nothing passes her; "the spiritual discerns all things, and he is discerned of no one", 1 Cor.2:15. She provides against this situation, takes her life in her hands, as it were, and the blessing goes to the right man in spite of Isaac's dullness.

REM: When fatherhood fails in a meeting the sisterhood may take it on.

JT: That is the point here. There are other instances too.

REM: Is Rebecca working this matter out for God according to what you spoke of as to the prophetic word in 1 Corinthians 14?

JT: It is clear that she is on that line. It so far is a very fine picture. She is a godly person and goes right through. It is now long after the boyhood period of her sons, but she carries the matter right through and saves the position, and brings Isaac into real fatherhood in the end.

J.Taylor, sr., Ministry Vol. 53, pgs. 445-448

In John 4 there is another instance of one who spoke of herself -- this time a woman. I have been thinking lately that we do not value the sisters sufficiently, nor do they themselves sufficiently value the place that they have with the Lord and the service that belongs to them. The New Testament abounds with evidence of the service that may be rendered by them. But then, too, a sister must speak as of herself; she has to speak from her own light and faith. This woman, it says, “left her waterpot”, which means that she had become spiritual. There was not the slightest reason why from the literal point of view she should not have taken that waterpot back full of water, but the fact that it is mentioned that she left it is to call attention to her spirituality. The Lord had said that the living water should become in her a fountain of water, and she had laid hold of the thought and so left her waterpot. I do not see that any sister can be of help unless she is spiritual. I do urge spirituality upon the sisters, and it is to the end that they might see the service that is available to them.

I would cite Deborah, a remarkable type of a woman whom God uses. She was the wife of Lapidoth, which means that she was the wife of a man who had light. There is significance in that. Many of our sisters have husbands who have light, but they must not live on the light of their husbands or they will not be of any use in the service of God. Deborah dwelt under the palm tree of Deborah; that is to say, she had acquired spiritual victory on her own account. It was her own palm tree. She dwelt under that, and hence it says Israel came up to her for judgment. I am afraid of anyone acquiring a reputation so that people seek them out -- they that are sought after and visited. I am afraid of that because the flesh can hardly stand it; yet it is possible, and with Deborah it was so. They came to her; there is no effort on her part to force things on people -- they came to her. I think she is a model for every sister. She dwelt under her own palm tree and her spiritual power among the saints was recognised.

J.Taylor, sr., Ministry Vol. 83 p.71

Paul was an exemplary Levite! He bore the saints of God in his heart. Levitical service is not limited to brothers; it is seen in the Scriptures in sisters as well. Phoebe was a "servant of the church", Romans 16:1, and Paul speaks of "women which laboured with me in the gospel", Philippians 4:3. There are many sisters now who are bearing things in prayer before God, and power and blessing in public ministry are, no doubt, often the fruit of this.

J. Taylor, sr., Ministry Vol. 2 p. 13

QUES. I suppose a godly sister can give a brother who is in the work very good advice sometimes, would you not think?

J.T. I know it to be so. What is to be discerned is that sisters have excellent instincts, better than men have; hence the importance of listening to their advice and of taking them into our confidence.

J. Taylor, sr., Ministry Vol. 17 p. 376

J.T. And so here, the Lord says, "Have ye understood all these things?". So we should be bent on understanding, and especially the sisters, because they are apt to assume that the brothers know everything and should know everything, whereas the sisters ought to know the truth too. There were prophetesses at the beginning, and there should be something of that kind today, if we are to have the truth clarified amongst sisters.

REM. "The elder to the elect lady and her children, whom I love in truth", 2 John 1.

J.T. And Phoebe too, at Rome.

J. Taylor, sr., Ministry Vol. 70 p. 206

The fact that the woman is commanded to keep silence in our assemblies might result in a lack of exercise; the sisters might lose the sense of exercise. But Scripture provides sisters with a great sphere, even for prophesying. You see how Priscilla, in her faith with her husband, was able to be useful, in her right place, to a great preacher like Apollos. If she takes her place in subjection, a woman may be used by God in a wonderful way. We have, in Anna, the formal title of prophetess, but she belonged to the old economy. It was the same with Miriam, and with Deborah. It is wonderful to see how Scripture holds us, so to speak, in balance; and the divine intention is that things with us should be in faith, in a living way, so that each sister may be available to the Holy Spirit. "All these things operates the one and the same Spirit, dividing to each in particular according as he pleases".

J. Taylor, sr., Ministry Vol. 27 p. 223

The disciples are able, too, to keep an appointment with the Lord, which shows the full effect of the teaching. The Lord had earlier told the disciples that after He was risen, He would go before them into Galilee (Matthew 26); in this chapter both the angel and the Lord told the women to tell the disciples to go into Galilee, where they would see Him. The apostles take the message from the sisters, but why did they not get it direct from the Lord, rather than from His messengers? The angel spoke to the women with authority: "Behold, I have told you". In Judges 13:7, the case of Manoah's wife, the angel spoke with the same authority. We find, in both instances, that sisters can convey the truth in a comely way. The women ran to bring His disciples word, and Jesus met them and saluted them. They were moving at the word of His messenger, and as doing so He meets them and greets them. Then He says, "Go, bring word to my brethren that they go into Galilee, and there they shall see me", Matthew 26:10. The Lord will use what is available. There were no brothers available, but the sisters were available, and He uses them to carry the message to His brethren. I think this service involves assembly influence; so that both brothers and sisters are brought under subjection to the Lord, and the disciples keep the appointment; verse 16.

J. Taylor, sr., Ministry Vol. 18 p. 424

QUES: Does that explain why she appears to be very free to a mere stranger as he is?

J.T.: I think so. She is seemly in every way; there is not a discrepancy in the whole proceeding, except in Laban. Everything is according to God, and all brings out the graces of the assembly, seen typically in this young woman. All is connected with the well, the use she makes of it, and her preparedness in view of this service.

REM: Peter speaks of showing hospitality to one another without grudging. I suppose that is a feature that is developed here.

J.T.: Yes; the liberality with which she acts; the man 'was astonished at her, remaining silent, to know whether Jehovah had made his journey prosperous or not' (v.21). What a beautiful spirit that is! And then it is said, "And it came to pass when the camels had drunk enough, that the man took a gold ring, of half a shekel weight, and two bracelets for her hands, ten shekels of gold, and said, Whose daughter art thou? Tell me, I pray thee. Is there room in thy father's house for us to lodge? And she said to him, I am the daughter of Bethuel the son of Milcah, whom she bore to Nahor" (v.22-24). Notice that! It is the sisterhood of the house of faith that is in mind. Typically, she understands that. It is to preclude any foreign mixture in marriage among believers. She is of the same family and line as Abraham. "And she said to him, There is straw, and also much provender with us; also room to lodge" (v.25). She does not even go in to ask her father, mother or brother. She is quite sure of her ground; that in her father's house can be furnished all that is needed for the servant of Abraham and his camels as well. "And the man stooped, and bowed down before Jehovah, and said, Blessed be Jehovah, God of my master Abraham, who has not withdrawn his loving-kindness and his faithfulness from my master; I being in the way, Jehovah has led me to the house of my master's brethren" (v.26-27). Well, we touch the top stone now; "my master's brethren"; and all centering in this young woman. It is a question of what culminates in the assembly.

J.Taylor, sr., Ministry Vol. 52 p. 62

He is ascending as a risen Man to His Father. What a great Person He is! To ascend is His own action, and Mary is to understand that she is not to touch Him, for He has not yet ascended (verse 17). Mary therefore shows that she has learned, and she goes to the disciples. The Lord gave her the message (verse 17), and she takes it, not as a teacher, for a woman does not teach men, and public teaching by women is not acceptable to God. We have this definitely set out in 1 Corinthians 14:34, and 1 Timothy 2:12. She is learning from Jesus how to act in a comely way, and she goes to the disciples saying that she "had seen the Lord, and that he had said these things to her". The Lord would instruct all sisters to be like her, comely in the assembly and in relation to saints generally.

The final word is about Mary of Bethany (chapter 12). The name of Mary has a spiritual significance. I believe it has to do with suffering, with bitterness. No one of us is of any value without having passed through bitter waters in our soul's history. The Lord Jesus is the true wood cast into the waters, making them sweet for her, and she is now a true worshipper of Jesus. She began to learn early. When Martha is criticising her, she is at school, learning as she sits at Jesus' feet. And now we have the grand result, for we never hear of her afterwards. She will shine in heaven, but here she shows how educated she is; she is the finished product. She knows what it is to be criticised, and criticism is one of the hardest things to bear. She experienced it from her sister, and now from the wicked Judas. Jesus says, She knows what she is doing, she has kept this for the day of My burial. She has the pound of ointment, which is very costly; spiritually it has cost her bitter experience. She is educated spiritually and has reached the thought of worship. She anoints Him with the ointment, and the house is filled with the odour. She wiped His feet with her hair -- she gives Jesus all the glory. She was ready for the opportunity and seized it as it came, and now she disappears, only to appear in the future in glory.

J.Taylor, sr., Ministry Vol. 41 p. 29

QUES. In a meeting where the only brother cannot read, is it right that a sister should read the Scriptures aloud?

J.T. It says, "Let your women be silent in the assemblies", so it is not right.

REM. But the sisters sing the hymns audibly with us.

J.T. We must always read Scripture in its setting. The silence in 1 Corinthians 14:34 obviously relates only to speaking and praying aloud, but not to singing, "for it is not permitted to them to speak; but to be in subjection". They were not to push themselves forward by speaking or praying aloud. During the singing the sisters have no occasion to bring themselves forward, for we all sing together.It says here, "It is a shame for a woman to speak in assembly", and nothing is said as to singing. One person speaks alone while the others listen, and the same applies also to praying. It is shameful for a sister to speak or to pray, and in this way to be the mouthpiece of the assembly. It is quite different with singing, for all who are present are singing. For the same reason the sisters can also say "Amen" after a prayer.

QUES. What should then an assembly do if the only brother cannot read?

J.T. That is an exceptional case, but we should not transgress the Scripture on that account. If a sister is to read anything aloud it is at a private meeting, but never at a gathering in the light of God's assembly. If the Lord has gathered the material, there will then be no such difficulties, there will be a brother there who can read.

QUES. Whom should a sister ask, who has no husband?

J.T. Such a sister is at a disadvantage. She is wholly cast upon the Lord and He will not forsake her. In 1 Corinthians 11:3, the man (that is, the male) is the head of the woman (that is, female). It does not mean there husband and wife, but male and female. Thus if a sister has not "her own husband" she can easily find a brother who as head will gladly instruct her. Everything is very plain if only we are simple. If a sister for example has an unconverted husband she can certainly not ask him. We are children of wisdom and it is contrary to wisdom to ask an unconverted person anything relating to the assembly. If a sister is to ask her own husband at home, it is presumed that he is converted and in fellowship. The apostle says, "I speak as to intelligent persons" (1 Corinthians 10:15), and we surely have enough intelligence to know what to do in such a case.

J.Taylor, sr., Ministry Vol. 77 p. 188

I pass on to John 12, so as to show how sisters come into this matter. I have been speaking of sisters: they were all there as the Spirit came, according to Acts 1 and 2. Now here is a great occasion, a supper made for Christ, and the place of it is suitably filled. We can understand there would be no vacant seats at this table. Martha served; that is, the idea of sitting is there, and the idea of serving is there. "Martha served" -- that is her part; and I suppose, service is never to cease; shall we not serve above? Jesus will; I mean, love would be active in that way, and nothing would be remiss, nothing wanting. No, dear brethren, love will never have anything that is not suitable, and everything needed is furnished.

So now it is a question of what this sister Mary can do. What has she got? One often feels, and surmises, without being severe on the sisters, that they do not think it necessary to have anything. As if they were saying, If the brothers have the things, let them give them out: we will receive them -- or maybe not receive them! Now the only one who, in the sense implied, had anything in this wonderful scene was Mary; and she had what was supremely suitable. She had it too, in the sense of preparation; it was something she had kept for some time; for what is any one of us if he has not spiritual history? Spiritual history is one of the greatest thoughts. Mary had spiritual history; she was not a believer of yesterday, she was a woman of spiritual history; Luke gives us the beginnings of it, John the finish. It is a fine piece of work, dear brethren! Would you not say, Well, I want to be a fine piece of work for heaven? Each one of us, I am sure, in our quiet, meditative moments wants to be a fine piece of work. Such divine workmanship is wonderful: "Let thy work appear unto thy servants", Psalm 90:16. Is there anyone here who would eliminate himself from that? Is the work of God not to appear in us? It is, even as it appeared in Mary. Luke gives us the beginnings, John the finish, as I said. This is the last mention of Mary in the Scriptures, though, of course, she has been mentioned millions of times since; there is no end to it at all. She has an eternal fame -- all in heaven will talk about Mary in the way I am speaking of her. She is a fine example of divine workmanship. She knows how to choose the good part -- to sit at the feet of Jesus and hear His word -- and now she has this ointment. It is very precious; she has kept it -- it does not say in an alabaster box, as elsewhere. The Spirit of God would eliminate that thought here. She kept it; she herself was the box. She was one of those who "love our Lord Jesus Christ in incorruption", Ephesians 6:24. You cannot corrupt her, in that sense; she is incorruptible. In principle and in result all true believers are; the first epistle of John views us in this abstract way; it is only a matter of the setting aside in time of all that is contrary. God looks at us abstractly, and there is the thought of it in a concrete way, seen in those who love our Lord Jesus Christ in incorruption, that is, to be entirely unselfish in it. So she kept the thing without an alabaster box; she was that herself. That is the way John presents Mary.

So the great occasion arrives, and there she is thoroughly in it and equal to it. She anoints the feet of Jesus. It is not an assembly occasion properly; for after the Lord discloses Himself to the assembly as such, to the persons who compose it, it is His hands and side of which He speaks; that is how John records the fact; but here it is the feet of Jesus. I suppose she represents the Jewish side; but still, we can include it amongst ourselves. It is a question of a journey, of six days yet to be traversed. She was waiting for His death, for the time of His burial, and it was a question of His feet. She is saying in effect, Those precious feet have travelled to me; they have to travel six days more; they have to travel to Golgotha, and I will express my love to Him whose feet they are! And she had the ointment; there was no need for self-complaint, saying, I wish I had brought that! What a fine opportunity it would be if I had it with me! Mary had it with her; it was herself in effect, dear brethren. There are things I may forget, but the point is what I am myself, that is the thing. She was there; the real Mary, the real workmanship of God was there; there was nothing wanting, no! She fitted there, as she will fit eternally. That is the idea in the assembly: I want to fit in there as a subject of the work of God, and to be ready for my opportunity. So the house is filled with the odour of the ointment.

J.Taylor, sr. Vol. 47 p. 361

You find at the end of the gospels examples of the Lord's confidingness. I refer, for a moment, to Matthew; you will remember how the Lord sent a message to His brethren by a sister, and I would remark, if you will allow me, that certain current references amongst us to sisters tend to divert them from their real calling and service. The Lord would, as it were, elevate them in their own minds as regards His service. We often say, 'Even a sister could do that'; but what is verified at the endings of the gospels is that the sisters are marked off as confided in, and so in this case the Lord sends a message to His disciples saying, "Go bring word to my brethren that they go into Galilee, and there shall they see me" Matthew 28:10.

J.Taylor, sr., Ministry Vol. 28 p. 92

A word given at a marriage meeting

"In the Lord" means that the natural will is superseded; that my will is not in it. It is the will of God. The authority of God is vested in the Lord Jesus, and hence marriage "in the Lord' implies that the will of God prevails, and not the natural wills of those entering into this relation.

We have here parents on both sides, true sons and daughters of Abraham, thank God, so that our dear brother and sister are well set out. Both have descended from right families, and the parental feelings to which I have alluded, exist. The wedding feast made by the king for his son, is reflected here; this is seen in what is provided for us here today; but then the thought now is that this parental principle should go down; that it should pass on. It is one of the greatest heritages that we have, the principles we have spoken of properly cherished and exercised in one generation, handed on to the next, all originating in God.

We have the right parents, and our young brother and sister are to cherish the principles in which they have been tutored, and in turn hand them down. It will be exercised in a variety of ways. It enters into the household, into entertainment of the saints, into hospitality generally, and into many other relations and circumstances.

J. Taylor, sr., Ministry Vol. 48 p. 377

Manoah's wife was more in it than he was and it is well that we should not forget that. It comes into Samson's history as well, as we see in chapter 14, and his father being mentioned by himself at times, would, I think, point to defectiveness in the position. It is necessary that the sisters should apprehend all this, so that they may not be onlookers, and simply followers of the brothers. They are to be fully in the truth, and there is no reason why they should not be. The Spirit of God makes much of women who have been leaders in the truth. Manoah's wife's name is never mentioned, but I think she represents the sisters as it says, "Let the women learn in silence". But she does not fail to meet a situation when it arises and to correct her husband.

J. Taylor, sr., Ministry Vol. 62 p. 85

J.T. Yes, and yet you can see how divine provision fitted exactly, so Joash is called the king, not merely the king's son. It is a great thing to nurse the kingly element, so that it becomes active. You get a remarkable correspondence in the Scriptures: so in Exodus 1, you have, "There arose a new king over Egypt, who did not know Joseph", and though Israel had no leader, they were fruitful and swarmed and multiplied. They were exposed to Pharaoh but women came forward and preserved the male side. Five women were used in this. The idea is that the subjective practical state among the brethren nurses what is of God. The seed royal is the child. You have the spiritual side in 2 Kings 11. Jehosheba is particularly to be noticed, as she comes in first; where women act, it is the subjective side that is prominent. So these five women in Exodus secure the male side, just as here Jehosheba takes the lead with the nurse: they hid the king's son. It says, "He was with her hid in the house of Jehovah six years". Then Jehoiada comes into view -- God would own the official side -- and acts throughout the chapter; thus the king is brought into evidence. It says Jehoiada "shewed them the king's son" (verse 4). Then verse 12: "And he brought forth the king's son, and put the crown upon him, and gave him the testimony; and they made him king, and anointed him; and they clapped their hands, and said, Long live the king!" The full thought is now reached, and this by way of the subjective line. Suppose there are two brothers in a gathering, and three times as many sisters; if the brothers have not gift, they have to be nursed, that is the idea. So the kingly side comes into evidence. We are never left at a loss. Over against Athaliah we have this woman acting for God.

REM. In Matthew we have "the little child and his mother".

J.T. The male side is in mind in Matthew, therefore Joseph is put in charge of the little child, but there is the mother; whereas Luke would enlarge on the female side, the birth of Christ, and the care manifested. It is a crisis here, a most precarious situation; it is all linked up with Jezebel. Jezebel would slay all the prophets, that is, the word and mind and authority of God, then you have apostasy. This chapter is intended to bring out the subjective side to meet conditions. If there is lack of lordship, subjective conditions may be relied on if God is working. In due course the priest comes in with the result, no longer the king's son but his being made king, the full position. The full divine position is reached, and yet he is a boy only seven years old, but he reigns the full time of David and Solomon, forty years. The complete idea of kingship is thus reached on these subjective lines.

It says in chapter 11: 2, "They hid him from Athaliah" -- whoever "they" were; that is the subjective state of things capable of hiding from the enemy what is of value. Then you get the moral result in the official side, the side God can own. The point is, that however small things may be, this state of soul can be relied upon. We want to bring in what is needed officially, not just to keep the meeting going. A sister would never arrogate authority but would indicate that it belongs to the king. The seventh year is full development.

REM. At Philippi women were prominent, assembling where prayer was wont to be made.

J.T. The male side was clearly indicated in the man of Macedonia, but the female stands out first, and as here, over against the female slave who was the tool of the enemy. Lydia attended to the things spoken by Paul, as Paul had the vision. The subjective side must get into touch with Paul, as Paul represents God. You get a murderous spirit in Acts, similar to what is found in Athaliah: God meets that by the subjective side in the assembly. The assembly comes into prominence in Acts almost immediately. It says of the Lord, "And, being assembled with them", Acts 1:4. The King was there but going away and the assembly was to occupy the ground.

Jehosheba did her work well, in relation to this principle of hiding. The secretive thought belongs to the subjective side, but when publicity comes in, there must be the king. The full thought is reached spiritually in the seventh year, so we have something designated as "The king", and he is to live long. Jehoiada fosters that, hence it is to his credit that in chapter 12 we have a king reigning forty years. His mother came from a covenant place. So you have a full spiritual product, the full position is in view as in David and Solomon. The priest and king (or, since David, king and priest) is the divine order. So if a meeting is weak, this describes what you get, as the priest is the development of a spiritual state in the woman, and that, in turn, develops into authority. Jehoiada is owned as introducing the king's son.

J.Taylor, sr., Ministry Vol. 86 p. 386

The next thing is aged women. There are a good many of them here today, too. What is said about them? "That the elder women in like manner be in deportment as becoming those who have to say to sacred things, not slanderers, not enslaved to much wine, teachers of what is right" (verse 3). It does not say here 'becoming sound doctrine', but 'sacred things'. How necessary that is in experienced women! "that they may admonish the young women to be attached to their husbands" (verse 4). There are a good many young women here. We may thank God for the young people that are married. It is an entire mistake to dissociate the marital idea from the testimony of God, it has a great place in that testimony. And the elder women are to be an example to the young women that are married: "not enslaved to much wine, teachers of what is right"; it is not a question of gift, it is a question of practical knowledge and moral power to be able to teach younger persons what is right in their spheres. "That they may admonish the young women to be attached to their husbands, to be attached to their children, discreet, chaste, diligent in home work, good, subject to their own husbands": first to love them, and then to be obedient to them, "that the word of God may not be evil spoken of" (verses 4, 5). See what is over against all these simple, practical things, that the elder women teach the younger ones; over against them, if these are not present, there will be blasphemy (verse 5). See how serious it is! Things may run riot where these things are disregarded. "Diligent in home work"; young people will never get any help in their souls in shopping. If you have to shop, of course, do it, but if you go into the shops for sight-seeing and spend a day there, you are sure to suffer. The authorised version says, 'keepers at home'. I think the word is 'workers at home'. I think the meaning of it is something like home work, as the children do, but that is work for school, done at home. But the wife -- her work is at home and do the work of the home. The old sisters are to teach that. You may say, This is too much detail, and too personal; but you see, this is Paul's letter to this trusted brother called Titus in the island of Crete, where the people are just as I have said, and where there is such exposure to corruption, and he is saying to Titus, You urge this matter of the old sisters and the young sisters.

J. Taylor, sr., Ministry Vol. 52 p. 329

Government in a Day of Small Things

Zechariah 6

As the question has been raised today as to the place sisters have in the service of God, the suggestion of a house enables one to enlarge on this point. The gospel of Luke prominently introduces women; it introduces them as priests, particularly Elizabeth, Mary and Anna. If any sisters wish to determine before God what their function is, what their service should be, I cannot advise them better than that they should read the Scriptures from the standpoint of the service and testimony of women as seen there. Take the gospel of Luke, as I said. The Lord arrives at Bethany, and a certain woman receives Him into her house. Is that not a service? Think of the honour of receiving Christ into your house! If you are set for that, you would be concerned for your house, for you are to guide it.

And we find that those who witnessed the Lord Jesus go up into heaven in Acts 1, returned to Jerusalem, and they go to an upper room, and it says, Peter, James and John were there ... and certain women. I think that upper room at Jerusalem was a place of general gathering, and what you observe is that certain women were there, amongst them the Lord's mother. These women would not be there listlessly. They would be there with keenest interest. They would follow all that passed. They would carry the burden of the testimony on their hearts. And then Mary the mother of Mark had a prayer meeting in her house. Then you find a girl, who, as the sequel shows, was in advance of them all. Her name was Rhoda. Is not that a word for young girls amongst us? She recognised Peter's voice. The others had prayed for him. Doubtless she had joined in the prayers, but she knew Peter's voice. They thought she was mad. You may get persecuted, young sister, but if you are true to Christ, the Lord will give you light, and you may shine more than others at times. Her name is given. It is an honour to have your name mentioned by God.

It is a great thing to be firm. If you know a thing is so, stand by it. Then again, you find a woman like Priscilla. What an honourable mention she has in Scripture! In Romans she is mentioned before her husband. This is not an accident, and what you find is that she and her husband had an assembly in their house. Do you not think that Priscilla would know what went on in that assembly? Earlier at Ephesus they had also an assembly in their house.

The prophet is here instructed to go the same day to the house of Josiah the son of Zephaniah. There is nothing said about women in that house, but undoubtedly there was a woman or women there. You see how God connects what is precious spiritually with the house. The most precious things are found in the houses of the saints, and I need not say again, the woman has to do with the house; it was so in connection with Peter. The Lord goes into the house and puts his mother-in-law right. He stands over her. And may I suggest that much that is wrong Christians is due to the insubjection of women? There is a want of authority in the man. The Lord, it is said, stood over her; Luke 4:39. As she would look up to Christ standing over her, she would be impressed with His authority. He rebuked the fever and it left her. Need any sister feel at a loss for her service? Peter's wife's mother did not have far to go. She arose and served them. And so again with Lydia, as the Lord opened her heart to attend to the things spoken by Paul, she opened her house to Paul and those that were with him.

J.Taylor, sr., Ministry Vol. 13 p. 6

QUES. This word of the prophetess Huldah was spoken to five men appointed by the king. Is it in order for a sister to speak to a few brothers what she believes to be the mind of God?

J.T. By all means; I have experienced that on more than one occasion, a sister conveying the mind of God. The Lord will give His mind to sisters if they ask for it. If sisters accept the general responsibility of the position and are before God about it they will get His mind. Why not? He will honour sisters as well as brothers. There are other principles that keep them from public speaking; nevertheless God uses sisters who cover their heads and recognise the authority above them. It is in subjection that they are used.

REM. I was thinking that the Lord sent the woman in John 20 to the brethren.

J.T. She went and told the disciples that she had seen the Lord and that He had said these things to her. She does not teach them; she conveys the word.

J.Taylor, sr., Ministry Vol. 81 p. 7

The Lord wants every brother and every sister to be called Cephas, so that persons understand that you yourself are contributing your own part to what is going on livingly in the assembly. Perhaps sisters may inquire how they contribute their part, seeing that they are not allowed to take part vocally in the assembly save in having part in the singing and in the amens, but they contribute their part just as really and as substantially as brothers, for they bring into the assembly affection for Christ, and affection for God the Father, and intelligence too, in the Spirit they bring in feelings and intelligence that are capable of being unified, in the power of the Spirit, with what is there with the rest of the brethren. In what is living they contribute much to the substance and wealth that is there, and every sister as well as every brother should recognise that this is why God has taken us up.

A.J.Gardiner volume "Piety and..." page 178

Well then, finally we have Deborah's song (for that is what is the theme of the chapter) -- "then sang Deborah", as you will observe, and Barak sang. This song is from victorious lips, triumphant lips, and the leader is a sister; the leader, too, in the great movement that overthrew the enemy. Deborah represents victory in sisters, beginning with victory over themselves, for she sat, as we are told, she judged Israel, dwelling under her own palm-tree -- the palm denoting undoubtedly her victory over herself. Otherwise how could she judge Israel? No true Israelite, viewed spiritually, would go to a person who is not self-judged, for judgment.

They came to her for judgment, we are told. Why did they do that? Because she was capable of judging. How had she become capable to judge? She had learned to judge herself, to acquire the victory over herself. "He that ruleth his spirit", we are told by the wise man, is better than he that takes a city. She did that, and she soon acquired a reputation among the spiritual for being capable of judging, and they came to her. We never need to advertise ourselves if we are self-judged. Those who advertise are conscious of the poverty of their commodity. It is as I am conscious of the wealth of my commodity that I use it, I know that those who need it will make a path to my door, and that is what they did to Deborah. A beaten path was made to that woman's door. Why? Because she was a self-judged person. They came to her for judgment and now she sings --

she and Barak. The chapter is well worth studying from this point of view, and it ends with this -- this beautiful note which I read: "Let them that love him be as the sun when he goeth forth in his might". What a figure that is! She had spoken directly to Jehovah. "So let all thine enemies perish, O Lord", she says. I did not read that part, for it is not now a time for calling down retribution on the enemies of God; it is the period of grace; but then we have, "let them that love him be as the sun". It is like a jewel inserted after the tribute, after the appeal to Jehovah in regard to His enemies. It is set beautifully, not in the address to Jehovah, but as to the saints -- to us -- "let them that love him", as if it were to stand out before us as a great thought throughout the ages, that those who love God are to shine as the sun in his might. What an incentive, dear brethren, to be amongst the lovers of God!

J.Taylor, sr., Ministry Vol.52 p. 406

Rem. In writing the first epistle to Corinthians the apostle connects a brother with him, and addresses the saints as brethren alluding to what had been shown him by the house of Chloe.

J.T. A very important matter that. Her house comes into it. We have mentioned others already who might be mentioned here too, showing the modifying influence of the sisters. How often it happens that brothers have a hard judgment about matters, and when they come home and talk about things with the sisters there is a modifying influence for good. So here you see David refers to the same thing, "Blessed be thy discernment, and blessed be thou, who hast kept me this day from coming with bloodshed, and from avenging myself with mine own hand". She, as it were, saved the position.

Rem. You mean, she prevented David from going too far?

J.T. How often that happens.

J.Taylor, sr., Ministry Vol. 58 p. 163

J.T. I think we have women's names given that would help us. It is a question of whether there is interest enough in the sisters to take the thing up There have been sisters who were peculiarly supported of God in relation to the teaching. They were very quiet and sober, but what they said carried weight. The question now is whether sisters are taking things on themselves, on moral lines, and doing things because there is that which has to be done.

QUES. How are we to understand the passage "The Lord gives the word: great the host of the publishers", Psalm 68:11. I understand the word 'publishers' is feminine. Does it mean the thought of the celebration of what is being spoken?

J.T. I would think the word 'publishing' would mean by word of mouth. You do not mean publishing in the sense of publishing books?

QUES. No, not at all. Publishing by word of mouth. Is it the thought of a celebration of victory in that sense?

J.T. Just so, because our mouths are to be used and our hands are to be used. There are other things we might say, but in this particular case, the sisters are clearly in mind. I think God would speak to all of us, and not simply to them, because the amount of help and labour afforded by the sisters amongst us is somewhat defective.

QUES. Would the service of the sisters have its place in the houses that are mentioned here? It says in verses 12 and 13, "And as ye enter into a house salute it. And if the house indeed be worthy, let your peace come upon it".

J.T. It says, "As ye enter into a house salute it". That is to say, the servants of God, in the carrying forth of their mission, are bound to come into the houses. So that readings in houses, for the setting out of the word of God, are evidently in mind, and the sisters can provide for that. But the twelve, in entering on their service, would enter into houses, and they would receive from the sisters in the houses. That would raise the question of the bringing up of young children, which is another great service that clearly should be in the hands of sisters. We have been speaking of the age at which children may come into fellowship, and how the influence of the mothers is to be there, so that the children should come into the truth and not be carried away with novels and other things in the schools.

QUES. Would Lydia's house and herself fit into that? She was a person with power, for Luke says, "she constrained us", Acts 16:15.

J.T. Yes. She had constraining power.

QUES. You were referring to the enriching of the service of God, through the influence of the sisters. Would Martha and Mary, in John 12, support that?

J.T. I think so. Earlier Martha had been cumbered with much serving, while Mary had sat at the Lord's feet, but in John 12 they are both happily in the service.

QUES. In Exodus 35 it says, "And every woman that was wise-hearted spun with her hands, and brought what she had spun: the blue, and the purple, and the scarlet, and the byssus. And all the women whose heart moved them in wisdom spun goats' hair". Would that bear upon what you are saying?

J.T. I think it would. Exodus fits in largely; it begins with sisters, and what they do, and sisters have a great place in what you are referring to.

J.Taylor, sr., Ministry Vo;. 70 p. 154

QUES. Would you say a word as to how sisters today have the privilege of making such a contribution as Mary's psalm?

J.T. Well, I think Mary is a model for sisters as Joseph is for brothers. Mary kept things in her mind and pondered them in her heart. I think she refers to the way sisters want to take things in and ponder them, and work things out from them. The more wealth they have in that way, the more the service of God will be added to. Because, here it is an experimental matter too; what God had done. She, herself, is a testimony to the great power of God in the most inscrutable way. It evidently alludes to spiritual formation and works out here in the readiness in which she has her part as seen in her composition. Elizabeth had hers too; the Holy Spirit came upon Elizabeth.

J.Taylor, sr., Ministrey Vol. 46 p. 437

Now this is a word for the sisters. Let us not forget that they also are to be leaders; they are to be led and they are to lead. Sisters lead in the sense of being examples. Nothing can be more important than sisterly example. How important that they should set a right example! The first epistle to Timothy speaks much of sisters; and in Titus, the elder women are to teach the young ones; they are to be before their eyes, yet they are to stand in relation to Moses and Aaron, so to speak; they are not to be independent. Miriam is not mentioned very often in Scripture; there is relatively very little mention of her; it is the fact that she was a sister of these great men that brings her into prominence. One mention of her is in the case of wrongdoing; that is a warning for sisters; she envied Moses and spake against him, a sorrowful matter! But I speak now, of what the Spirit of God has in mind in a trio like Moses, Aaron and Miriam, sent before the brethren, before the sisters, "I sent before thee Moses, Aaron, and Miriam".

Well now, the first mention we get of Miriam by name is in Exodus 15, and she had influence with the other sisters. One might say much about the prophetesses of Scripture; one has indeed spoken of them; but what is to be said about Miriam shows that she had influence with the other sisters in Israel, they followed her. It says, "Miriam the prophetess, the sister of Aaron, took the tambour in her hand, and all the women went out after her with tambours and with dances" (Exodus 15:20). A very fine example as representing the sisterly side! And when I say the sisterly side, I have in mind the subjective state of the saints, that which is connected with the interests of the young and of all, what there is for God in that sense. So that you find in a house like that of Philip the evangelist four daughters that prophesied. They are brought in as Paul is journeying to Jerusalem; what an atmosphere would mark that house! It is a question of that kind of thing amongst us, dear brethren, as outstanding, for it is a question of going before. They are there before, as it were; God sent them before. So if a sister prophesies or prays, there is much said about it, and what is said about the order is intended to tax her spirituality. We shall never come to the end of that passage in 1 Corinthians 11, but it is to tax our spirituality, as to whether we are subject, as to whether we are ready to go out of the way in the disregard of natural things; otherwise the spirit of prophecy is beclouded.

J.Taylor, sr., Ministry Vol. 79 p. 109

Exodus 2:1-14; Exodus 3:1-10; Exodus 4:27-31

I want now to speak of the elect lady and her children; it is a remarkable expression. "The elder to the elect lady and her children, whom I love in truth; and not I only, but also all who have known the truth". 2 John 1:1. Now Peter uses a similar expression in 1 Peter 5:13; and we all know how Paul respects sisters, respects those who serve in truth, as in the case of Phoebe, and Lydia, and others; and indeed the Scriptures throughout signalise persons called "holy women", beginning with Sarah, then Rebecca, and right down to such as Deborah, Abigail, and many others. How the Spirit of God signalises them as having a public place in the testimony; not simply for doing the ordinary service of sisters or women, but as engaged in actual testimony; and this sister called "the elect lady" is amongst them, and she has another sister, for John says to her, "The children of thine elect sister greet thee". 2 John 1:13. She had another sister who was also elect; that is, distinguished. Then Peter says to the saints, "She that is elected with you in Babylon salutes you". 1 Peter 5:13. The Authorised Version says "The church", but the Darby Translation says, "She that is elected with you". It is remarkable that these two apostles have sisters in their minds; and then, as I said, what a place Paul gives sisters in his epistles. I need say nothing about 1 Corinthians, and 2 Corinthians, and then Philippians; these evidence what I am saying, what place sisters have in the testimony; not doing simply the ordinary daily household duties of sisters, but serving in testimony so as to acquire distinction, as I might say, in heaven. We have in Paul's first epistle to Timothy a sister who is to be put on the list. That is remarkable, and her history is to be known, what qualities she had, what services she rendered; so with many others. Sisters are not only honoured in doing their ordinary duties, but serving in the testimony, and therefore I venture to launch out a little on this point, and having already delivered my soul in connection with the first passage read, I now turn to this epistle as to the elect lady and her children.

As I was saying, Peter has the same sort of thing in mind, and we cannot think that, in what he says about sisters, he includes their marital relations; he speaks about what is in their hearts, the hidden man of the heart. I would specially mention that, "the hidden man of the heart, in the incorruptible ornament of a meek and quiet spirit which in the sight of God is of great price". 1 Peter 3:4. I would specially refer to what sisters have in their hearts, and the loyalty that belongs to it, and the graciousness that becomes those who profess to belong to the assembly; so that the hidden man of the heart is there. The assembly must be in Peter's mind, it is not as if he spoke of it in the marital relation, but it clearly is in his mind, as also in John's, and in Paul's. Therefore all these remarks as to sisters must originate in the first chapter of the Bible. It is a question of what is in the mind of God to bring about eternally and in testimony here for the little while that remains to us while we are here.

J.Taylor, sr., Ministry Vol. 60 p.161

www.ingramcontent.com/pod-product-compliance
Lightning Source LLC
LaVergne TN
LVHW091010080826
845145LV00003B/1214

* 9 7 8 0 9 1 2 8 6 8 2 4 0 *